Elements in Islam and the Sciences
edited by
Nidhal Guessoum
American University of Sharjah, United Arab Emirates
Stefano Bigliardi
Al Akhawayn University in Ifrane, Morocco

MUSLIM WOMEN IN SCIENCE, PAST AND PRESENT

Elmira Akhmetova
University of Freiburg

Shaftesbury Road, Cambridge CB2 8EA, United Kingdom

One Liberty Plaza, 20th Floor, New York, NY 10006, USA

477 Williamstown Road, Port Melbourne, VIC 3207, Australia

314–321, 3rd Floor, Plot 3, Splendor Forum, Jasola District Centre,
New Delhi – 110025, India

103 Penang Road, #05–06/07, Visioncrest Commercial, Singapore 238467

Cambridge University Press is part of Cambridge University Press & Assessment,
a department of the University of Cambridge.

We share the University's mission to contribute to society through the pursuit of
education, learning and research at the highest international levels of excellence.

www.cambridge.org
Information on this title: www.cambridge.org/9781009539425

DOI: 10.1017/9781009418515

© Elmira Akhmetova 2025

This publication is in copyright. Subject to statutory exception and to the provisions
of relevant collective licensing agreements, no reproduction of any part may take
place without the written permission of Cambridge University Press & Assessment.

When citing this work, please include a reference to the DOI 10.1017/9781009418515

First published 2025

A catalogue record for this publication is available from the British Library

ISBN 978-1-009-53942-5 Hardback
ISBN 978-1-009-41852-2 Paperback
ISSN 2754-7094 (online)
ISSN 2754-7086 (print)

Cambridge University Press & Assessment has no responsibility for the persistence
or accuracy of URLs for external or third-party internet websites referred to in this
publication and does not guarantee that any content on such websites is, or will
remain, accurate or appropriate.

Muslim Women in Science, Past and Present

Elements in Islam and the Sciences

DOI: 10.1017/9781009418515
First published online: March 2025

Elmira Akhmetova
University of Freiburg

Author for correspondence: Elmira Akhmetova, eakhmetova@gmail.com

Abstract: This Element examines issues related to Muslim women's engagement in science and scholarship, both past and present. The first two sections discuss the contributions made by Muslim women to scholarly, scientific, and technological advancements. The third section discusses the factors that have contributed to a decline in Muslim women's scholarly involvement in Islamic civilisation, the veracity of historical accounts, and the constraints in original knowledge production in contemporary Muslim societies. It finds that there are no religious restrictions rooted in the Qur'an that forbid women from pursuing a profession in science, whether as learners or practitioners. Yet some economic and political circumstances, cultural influences, and outdated interpretations of Islam produce discrimination against women in Muslim societies and lead to their underrepresentation in scientific research and academia.

Keywords: Muslim women in science, women in Islamic history, Muslim female scientists, science in Islam, gender disparity in the Muslim world

© Elmira Akhmetova 2025

ISBNs: 9781009539425 (HB), 9781009418522 (PB), 9781009418515 (OC)
ISSNs: 2754-7094 (online), 2754-7086 (print)

Contents

1 Introduction   1

2 A Historical Survey of Muslim Women's Contributions to the Sciences   8

3 Contemporary Muslim Women in Sciences   19

4 Muslim Women and Science-Related Issues   30

5 Conclusion   50

    References   55

1 Introduction

Numerous studies have discussed women's participation in scientific developments from diverse cultural and ideological viewpoints (Cook, 1997; Allred, 2016; Gaida, 2016; Dajani et al., 2021). These studies generally suggest that, up until the late eighteenth century, women's contributions to science were minimal to nearly zero because of the predominant pre-modern perceptions of women as sole agents for reproduction who were intellectually and physically incapable of science and knowledge production. Men, viewing science as a 'masculine' activity, systematically excluded women from the field in medieval and early modern Europe (Allred, 2016, p. 14).

Along similar lines, the status of women in Islam and their contributions to societal and scientific developments are particularly attention-grabbing subjects in contemporary academia, public culture, the media, and Islamic studies. The discourse surrounding women and Islam is a relatively recent phenomenon, originating from the era of colonialism and the Western-led endeavours to modernise governments through the culture and ideology of the nation state (Sonbol, 2003, p. 3). Hence, this discourse mostly studies this issue from contemporary gender equality and Western cultural perspectives, while frequently disregarding historical realities and context, as well as distinctive cultural considerations.

As a part of the Cambridge Elements in Islam and the Sciences, this Element, titled *Muslim Women in Science, Past and Present*, explores the relationship between sciences and women from an Islamic perspective. Women's inadequate status in the modern Muslim world and their scarce participation in academia and scientific advancements have been the focus of debates at the crossroads of the twenty-first century. According to previous studies, 'at the global level, Muslim women are less educated and have wider gender gaps than all other religious groups except Hindus' (Mcclendon, Hackett, Potančoková, Stonawski, Skirbekk, 2018, p. 1). While discussing inadequate participation of Muslim women in STEM, John Esposito, a prominent contemporary scholar of Islamic studies, stated that 'A commonly accepted belief, fostered by the existence of such practices as the veiling (*burqa*) and seclusion (*purdah*) of women, is that Islam is a religion that grants no rights to women but rather prescribes their total subjugation to men' (Esposito, 1975, p. 100).

Hence, this Element aims to examine the historical and contemporary contributions made by Muslim women to scientific and technological advancements, knowledge generation, and dissemination. Overall, the discussions generally centre on the presumptions and stereotypes that are prevalent today in the context of women, science, and Islam such as: (1) Islam forbids women from participating in public life, including educational and scientific pursuits; (2) in the Muslim past, similar to medieval Europe, women were completely denied access to education and knowledge due to their presumptive biological traits as emotional beings and an 'inherently lusty' mindset without cognitive abilities; and (3) modern religious Muslim women are barely engaged in scientific and technological developments as such activities are not permissible in Islam.

1.1 Women in Islam

The sacred book of Muslims, the Qur'an, as well as the tradition (*sunnah* or *ḥadīth*, i.e., sayings and actions) of the Prophet Muhammad indicate equity and parity between men and women. The idea that men and women have been created of the same source with the same attributes was revealed in chapter (*sūrah*) al-Zumar: 'He created you from a single being; then of the same kind made its mate' (The Qur'an, *al- Zumar* 39:6).

Furthermore, numerous passages from the Qur'an affirm that women have the same rights and obligations as males in the sight of God. As observed by Esposito, the Qur'an declared 'women's religious equality with men both as regards their obligation to pray and lead virtuous lives and their equality of rewards and punishments at the final judgement' (Esposito, 1975, p. 104). For instance, in chapter *al-Muddathir*, it is clearly stated: 'Every soul will be (held) in pledge for its deeds' (The Qur'an, *al-Muddathir* 74:38). On another occasion, the Qur'an articulates: 'Whosoever does good, whether male or female, and is a believer, these will enter the Garden; they will be provided therein without measure' (The Qur'an, *al-Mu'min* 40:40). Therefore, whether in the worldly life or the Hereafter, men and women are equal recipients of God's favour and bounty.

The most significant social change brought about by Islam in the seventh century was the transition from tribal societies to a family-based social structure. Therefore, the Qur'an concentrated on modifying customary law by elevating the status of women in Islam in order to enhance the family in Muslim culture. The three basic components of family law – marriage, divorce, and inheritance – were improved by the Qur'anic reforms (Esposito, 1975, p. 103).

As an Australian-born British scholar on Islam, Charis Waddy perceived Islam to be 'an egalitarian creed. Whatever the localised social inequalities, it preaches the dignity of each human soul, a man and woman alike' (Waddy, 1980, p. 5). Islam's fundamental tenet is that men and women should complement one another to achieve mutual fulfilment. Family life is not built on a formal hierarchy of rights and responsibilities. Rather, the foundations of the husband-wife and parent-child relationships in Islam are *sakīnah* (peace, restfulness, and honour), *mawaddah* (affection), *raḥmah* (forgiveness, grace, mercy, compassion), and *rifq* (gentleness).

The Prophet in his Last Sermon advised his companions accordingly:

> O People, it is true that you have certain rights with regard to your women, but they also have rights over you. Remember that you have taken them as your wives only under Allah's trust and with His permission. If they abide by your right then to them belongs the right to be fed and clothed in kindness. Do treat your women well and be kind to them for they are your partners and committed helpers. And it is your right that they do not make friends with any one of whom you do not approve, as well never to be unchaste. (McIntire, 2009, p. 79)

According to Islamic law (Sharī'ah), women are entitled to independent property ownership. Islamic law completely recognises a woman's right to own her own wealth and assets, whether married or not. Women maintain the right to own property and can buy, sell, mortgage, or lease their properties without their husbands' consent, even after being married (Akhmetova, 2015, p. 60). The Qur'an also established women's right to inherit (The Qur'an, Al-Nisā' 4: 11–14). This ruling was revolutionary for seventh-century society as women in the Arabian Peninsula and some other cultures were not allowed to inherit and were completely dependent on male relatives. Women's shares stipulated in the Qur'an are less than men's (the general principle is that male heirs receive a share that is twice that of female heirs), yet, the new inheritance regulation ensured that women would have some financial security and rights in a familial and societal context (Esposito, 1975, p. 104).

Additionally, Islamic teaching does not prevent women from seeking employment, although maintaining that their roles as mothers and wives are blessed and crucial. The areas in which women can acquire their skills and knowledge are also unrestricted (al-Mawardi, 1966, p. 65). The Qur'an, the *sunnah*, and the consensus of the scholars (*ijma'*) do not include any ruling that denies women the ability to participate in public life or politics. Women were certainly involved in public life during the time of the Prophet. A few centuries later, some restrictions such as *burqa* or seclusion were imposed on women due to specific circumstances of that time, yet these customs were never commanded under the Sharī'ah as normative or unquestionably acceptable.

Both during and after the Prophet's lifetime, when Islamic civilisation was thriving, a long line of female intellectuals and activists acquired high positions and significant reputations (Kamali, 2002, p. 69). For instance, the Prophet appointed women to key administration positions. He assigned Samra binti Nuhaik al-Asadīyyah to the position of *muḥtasib* (market inspector), where she oversaw commercial operations and guarded the general welfare. After the death of the Prophet Muhammad, Samra continued serving in this office throughout the reigns of the first two caliphs, Abū Bakr and 'Umar. When

Samra passed away, the caliph 'Umar appointed another female to the same position, al-Shifā (Layla) binti 'Abdullah (Bisati, 2016, p. 37; Ahmad et al., 2020, pp. 328–329). She rose to prominence in her society and won great regard for her morality, piety, and knowledge. These are many more examples in which women participated actively in the political, economic, and educational arenas during the early Islamic period.

To sum up, in the seventh century, Islam liberated women from ignorance and various forms of gender-based prejudices that were pervasive in pre-Islamic societies. Historically, compared to the situation in pre-Islamic societies, Islam has improved the status of women and provided them with better access to social and educational possibilities. A renowned Scottish historian and orientalist known for his expertise in Islamic and Arab history, William Montgomery Watt, suggested that the Prophet Muhammad in this manner 'can be seen as a figure who testified on behalf of women's rights'.[1] The Qur'an and the Prophet's actions espoused equity and parity between men and women in both private and public life while upholding the distinctive roles that each gender plays in marriage, family, and society.

1.2 Women, Knowledge, and Science

The Qur'an highly recommends using common sense and reason in seeking the truth and criticises those who make assertions that are not supported by knowledge and reason or who blindly follow in the footsteps of their ancestors: 'Indeed, the worst of living creatures in the sight of Allah are the deaf and dumb who do not use reason' (The Qur'an, *al-Anfāl* 8:22).

According to the Islamic perspective, a human being's superiority over all other beings, even angels, is determined by his or her level of knowledge. For instance, a discussion between God and the angels over the former's choice of Adam as His vicegerent (*khalīfah*) on earth can be found in the Qur'anic chapter titled *al-Baqarah* (The Cow). Nonetheless, the angels expressed their scepticism about human's capacity for carrying out this task, asking, 'Will You place upon it [the earth] one who causes corruption therein and sheds blood, while we declare Your praise and sanctify You?' God retorted, 'I know that which you do not know' (The Qur'an, *al-Baqarah* 2:30). Then, God taught Adam the 'names of all things', which, according to Qur'anic exegetes, refers to knowledge of the nature of all things. The angels consequently bowed down before Adam in appreciation of his superior knowledge.

---

[1] Maan, B. & McIntosh, A. (2000). *The Whole House of Islam, and We Christians with Them: An Interview with the 'Last Orientalist' the Rev Prof William Montgomery Watt*, www.alastairmcintosh.com/articles/2000_watt.htm.

Muslims in the early days of Islam explored nature as a means of deciphering both the signs of God and the Divine code upon which the cosmic order was based. The Islamic world view held that science consequently operated within a moral and religious context. The Muslims' integrative approach that did not establish any distinction between the religious sciences and the natural or worldly sciences inspired them to thrive in a variety of disciplines. Early Muslims upheld a unified epistemology that combined science, technology, and spirituality, which Osman Bakar, a contemporary Malaysian scholar on Islamic philosophy and science, refers to as a God-centric world view that was governed by the Qur'an (Bakar, 2008, pp. 88–89).

In actuality, it was the development of the experimental method that distinguished Islamic civilisation from prior civilisations. Rationalist Greek thinkers like Plato discredited the study of reality. Aristotle, though not scientific by modern standards, was more strongly inclined to observe and describe reality. Islam emerged as a religion that emphasises reasoning, knowledge, and observation, which are the key components needed for scholarship and scientific advancement. Muslims were continuously urged by the Prophet Muhammad to seek knowledge, reflect, and contemplate on natural occurrences to better appreciate God's might and wisdom. This mentality contributed to Islamic civilisation's dominance of science for approximately 600 years. Muslim scholars believed that revelation, *sunān* Allāh (natural laws of the universe), *fitrah* (inborn intuition), and, most importantly, observation of these natural laws were the main sources of knowledge. They did not minimise the power of reason, but they acknowledged its limitations. This perspective led to the development of an experimental approach as early as the ninth century. For instance, Ibn al-Haytham (965–1040), a scholar from Basra (modern-day Iraq) who was known in the West by his Latinised name Alhacen or Alhazen, is acknowledged as one of the most eminent physicists during the pre-modern era due to his contributions in the field of optics and the establishment of experiments as the standard of proof in the field. His book – *Kitāb al-Manāzir* (The Book of Optics), translated into Latin as *De Aspectibus* – impacted early-modern European thinkers, including Roger Bacon, Johannes Kepler, Galileo, and Newton (Lindberg, 1967, pp. 321–341; Gorini, 2003, pp. 53–55).

Furthermore, Muslims pioneered the provision of basic public education because of the importance Islam placed on knowledge, regardless of gender or social class. For instance, mosques frequently provided primary education to both boys and girls during the early Islamic era. For a society to be sustainable, vigorous, and advanced, women's education is as necessary as that of males. The pursuit of knowledge was therefore encouraged for both men and women, even though it was not always possible in pre-modern Muslim societies. Islam views education as a duty of every human being, devoid of distinctions based on gender, ethnicity, or religion (Bsoul, 2018, pp. 13–14). Great Muslim scholars emerged from a civilisation that was founded on such Islamic knowledge-oriented attitudes. During the age of productivity in Islamic civilisation, participation in scientific pursuits affected all social classes equally, irrespective of their gender, ethnicity, or religious beliefs.

In general, there is no religious law that forbids women from pursuing a career in science (Sonbol, 2003, p. 6). However, compared to men, the number of women who are recognised as inventors in scientific and technological development is considerably smaller. The history books that recorded the names of those who excelled in science and discovery mentioned almost no Muslim women (Afsaruddin, 2002, p. 461). In contrast to the natural sciences, however, there is a wealth of material about Muslim women's contributions to religious studies. Medieval Arabic writings and biographical accounts list numerous female experts who have had a significant influence on the development and application of *ḥadīth* studies, theology, and *fiqh* dating back to the early days of Islam. After the death of the Prophet in 632, his wives 'Aisha bint Abū Bakr and Umm Salama (Hind bint Abu Umayya), his daughter Fāṭima, and many other educated female companions, including Khirat bint Abu Hadrad al-Aslāmī (also known as Ummu Dardā' al-Kubra), Asma bint Yāzid ibn Sakan al-Ansarīyyah, and Fāṭimah bint Qays, were consulted by the Muslim community, including scholars, as some of the main experts in establishing Islamic judicial verdicts and norms (Al-'Asqalani, 1968, vol. 13, p. 40; Abou-Taleb, 2012, p. 94). The male scholars in jurisprudence repeatedly consulted these women to clarify confusing legal matters like inheritance, female legal issues, family law, and the Islamic criminal code. These female scholars were qualified to issue legal rulings (*fatwah*) on matters of Islamic law (*Sharī'ah*) in response to various issues raised by other people, judges, or even government officials because of their vast knowledge of the Qur'anic verses and oral tradition of the Prophet (*ḥadīth*).

A careful reading of biographical dictionaries and historical sources reveals a large number of women who are classified as *faqīhāt* (female jurists) and who 'attained a level of competence that qualified them to issue fatwas' (Abou El Fadl, 2003, p. 40). Shihāb al-Dīn al-Asqalanī mentions the name Zayn al-'Arab bint 'Abd Raḥmān b. 'Umar b. al-Ḥussain (d. 1304) who occupied a prestigious teaching chair in Makkah (al-Asqalani, 1997, vol. 2, p. 69). Abou El Fadl suggests that 'The stories of these women jurists are enormously diverse, and they suggest venues of research that might lead to the reconstruction of the understanding of gender relations in Islamic legal history' (Abou El Fadl, 2003, p. 40).

In addition to their contributions to jurisprudence, Muslim women were essential in the development and preservation of *ḥadīth* from the beginning of Islam and many of them were renowned scholars who made significant contributions to the field of *ḥadīth* and related subjects (Hambly, 1999, pp. 8–9). Abundant information on women's participation in *ḥadīth* transmission can be found in biographical dictionaries, *ḥadīth* collections, chronicles, and diplomas (*ijāzāt*) (Haredy, 2020, p. 908). 'Aisha bint Abū Bakr, who transmitted a wealth of knowledge about Muhammad and is now regarded as the foremost authority in Islam on issues pertaining to women's roles, was crucial to the growth, development, and comprehension of Islam. Ibn Sa'd listed over twenty women in his *al-Tabaqāt* as authoritative *ḥadīth* narrators in the section on common women (Ibn Sa'd, 1957, vol. 8, pp. 169, 176, 179; Abou-Taleb, 2012, pp. 140–142).

Notable female *ḥadīth* scholars from the *tabi'īn* (the third generation of Muslims who were the students of the Prophet's companions, or *ṣaḥāba*) included 'Umra bint 'Abd al-Raḥmān, who was 'Aisha's student and secretary, and about whom the Umayyad caliph, 'Umar ibn 'Abd al-'Azīz (r. 717–720), said that he knew of no one alive who was more knowledgeable in the *ḥadīth* of 'Aisha than 'Umra (Ibn Sa'd, 1957, vol. 8, p. 331; Abou-Taleb, 2012, pp. 141–142); Umm al-Darda Sughrah (d. 700), a prominent jurist from Damascus considered to be superior to prominent *ḥadīth* scholars like Ibn Sīrīn and Ḥasan al-Basrī, and a jurisprudence teacher of the Umayyad caliph 'Abd al-Malīk ibn Marwan (r. 685–705); Hafsah bint-Sīrīn, a student of Anas ibn Malik; A'bida Al-Madaniyah (eighth-century scholar), a freed slave and wife of the Spanish *ḥadīth* scholar Habib Duhan; and Fāṭima Al-Batayahiyyah, a well-known scholar of the eighth century who taught *Saḥīḥ Bukhari*, one of the most important *ḥadīth* collections, in Damascus to leading male scholars of that time (Cornell, 2007, p. 138). 'Aisha bint Sa'd ibn Abī Waqqās was another knowledgeable woman in Islamic studies from this generation, and she became a teacher to several eminent jurists and *ḥadīth* scholars, including Imam Malik (711–795), Hakim ibn 'Utaybah, and Ayyub al-Sakhtiyani (d. 748).

There were many female scholars who taught in the mosque-universities and their learning earned them high recognition from their male colleagues and a large number of students. For example, Shuhda bint al-'Ibari (d. 1178) earned the title of 'the glory of women' and rose to become one of the most renowned intellectuals of her age. Due to her extensive knowledge of the religious sciences, she attracted many students in Baghdad (Esposito, 1975, p. 105). Zaynab bint 'Umar Al-Kindi of Damascus was another prominent Muslim scholar who lived in the late thirteenth and early fourteenth centuries. Taj al-Dīn al-Subki (d. 1355), al-Dhahabi (d. 1348), and Ibn-Battuta (d. 1369) were among her students. She taught subjects related to *ḥadīth* studies at the madrasas of Damascus. Numerous *isnads* (chains of *ḥadīth* transmitters) by Ibn Hajar al-Asqalānī (d. 1448) contain her name (Nadwi, 2013, p. 117).

Haredy mentions the example of Umm al-Khayr Fāṭima bt. Ibrahīm b. Muḥammad b. Jawhar al-Ba'labakkī (d. 711/1311) – one of the women in the classical age of Islam who held classes in mosques. She used to teach *ḥadīth* in the mosque of the Prophet in Madina (Haredy, 2020, p. 913). Ibn Rushayd narrated about her accordingly: 'She came in the Syrian caravan as a visitor and pilgrim. I met her in the mosque of the Prophet and *ḥadīth* was read to her while she was leaning on the side of the wall of the grave of the Prophet in front of his head. She wrote an *ijāza* with her own hand for me and for others' (Berkey, 1992, p. 179).

Kitāb al-Fihrist of Ibn al-Nadīm (d. 998) mentions a number of women who were politically influential and actively involved in the Abbasid communities of the time with a varied range of talents and expertise, particularly as poets (Waddy, 1980, p. 70). Many women in the literary profession attained a prominent reputation in Muslim Spain as well. Scott mentions several prominent names of Andalusian women who excelled in poetry, rhetoric, and the oratory arts such as Ayesha (d. ca. 1010), the daughter of Prince Ahmed; Wallada bint al-Mustakfi (ca. 1010–1087 or 1095), a princess of the Almohades; Algasania and Safia from Seville; and Miriam, the gifted daughter of Al-Faisuli, who lived in the first half of the eleventh century (Scott, 1904, vol. 3, p. 447). Another talented Andalusian poetess known for her literary skills and knowledge of Arabic grammar was Hafsa bint al-Hajj al-Rukuniyya, who died in 1190 (Borgerson, 2021, p. 83; Kudsieh, 2003, pp. 10–15). She actively engaged in intellectual discussion and scholarly circles, where her opinions and contributions were highly valued. Her participation in these gatherings raised the intellectual atmosphere of the time and enhanced her standing as a respected scholar.

Hence, the body of knowledge pertaining to the contributions of Muslim women in the realms of education, religion, and literature is notably comprehensive compared to the relative paucity of information concerning their pursuits in the scientific domain. Therefore, the primary objectives of this booklet are to illuminate the contributions of Muslim women to scientific advancement throughout history up to contemporary times, while also examining the causes for their underrepresented status in the field of science.

2 A Historical Survey of Muslim Women's Contributions to the Sciences

Between the ninth and as late as the sixteenth centuries, the most important hubs for studying what we today call the 'natural sciences' were in the Islamic world. During that time, the term 'science' did not convey its precise contemporary meaning; rather, its scope included the 'mathematical sciences of arithmetic, geometry, and trigonometry, and their applications in various fields such as astronomy, astrology, geography, cartography, and optics' (Hogendijk & Sabra, 2003, p. vii). The Islamic world experienced an 'age of scientific growth and discovery' (Al-Andalusi, 2015, p. 229).

In line with these discussions, our main purpose is to look into the specific role played by Muslim women in intellectual and scientific development. Hence, this historical survey concentrates on Muslim women's contributions to the exact sciences during the Islamic era, particularly in the domains of mathematics, medicine, and astronomy.

At the same time, we recognise the scarcity of materials for determining the concrete realities of women's lives and scholarly achievements during the early period of Islamic history. Islamic religious texts such as the Qur'an and the *ḥadīths* of Muhammad contain the most important information for studying women in early Islam. Islamic biographical dictionaries, known as *ṭabaqāt*, include a substantial amount of information about women, mostly the female companions of the Prophet. For instance, from the 4,250 biographies mentioned in the earliest biographical collection, *Kitāb al-Ṭabaqāt* by Ibn Sa'd (d. 230/845), 629 are devoted to women (Roded, 2003, p. 29). Other biographical works such as *Tarīkh Madīnat Dimashq: Tarājim al-Nisā'* by Ali b. al-Ḥasan ibn Asākīr (d. 571/1176), *Ṣifāt al-Ṣafwah* by 'Abd al-Rahmān al-Jawzī (d. 597/1201), *Tadhkirat al-Awliya* by Farīd al-Dīn 'Aṭṭār (d. 628/1230), and *al-Iṣāba fī Tamyīz al-Ṣaḥāba* by al-'Asqalānī (d. 852/1449) have sections on women who were contemporaries of the Prophet. Asma Afsaruddin, a contemporary American scholar of Islamic studies, categorises the women recorded in the historical biographical dictionaries into four principal groups: (1) relatives and contemporaries of the Prophet; (2) transmitters of *ḥadīth*; (3) female mystics and women of learning in general; and (4) women of literary and cultural accomplishments (Afsaruddin, 2003, pp. 32–33). Nevertheless, not much information is available in Muslim historiographic tradition related to the role of women in the natural sciences.

2.1 Muslim Women in the Field of Exact Sciences

Scholarship on women and science in pre-modern Muslim societies has advanced very little. While speaking about the history of science in the Islamic world, an expert in the history of women's healthcare in pre-modern Europe, Monica H. Green, acknowledged: 'The historiography of science and medicine in the Islamic world has a long pedigree, stretching back to the medieval biographical dictionaries of such writers as Ibn Abi Usaybia. To my knowledge, no female scientists or healers appear in these biographical dictionaries' (Green, 2003, p. 358). In recent years, a few names of Muslim women scientists have surfaced, but they all date to the tenth century (Keddie, 1990, p. 91; Gaida, 2016, p. 197). The first name among them that we are aware of is associated with the study of astronomy and the art of creating astrolabes.

Astrolabes are astronomical devices that are thought to have been invented by the Greeks before the Common Era (Schmidl, 2016, p. 179), and were perfected and popularised throughout the Islamic world. The astrolabe had five circles of copper: 'the half-day circle, the zodiac circle, the viewing circle, the tilt circuit, and the solar circuit known as the planetary system' (Bsoul, 2018, p. 170). Astrolabes were the most advanced form of portable technology in pre-modern societies until the first pocket clocks started to appear in the sixteenth century. It was a crucial tool for astronomers to position the stars, calculate latitude, and determine the precise time. The application of astrolabes was particularly extensive and religiously critical in the Islamic world because it was essential to calculate accurate times for the five daily prayers, which change daily and vary in different geographical locations due to changes in the position of the sun, as well as to determine the *qibla* (the direction towards the Kaaba in Makkah, Saudi Arabia, that Muslims face while performing prayers). As a result, historically, most large mosques contained time-keeping rooms with astrolabes to determine the precise time of each prayer. Muslim travellers and traders were also interested in possessing this device to use for a variety of travelling-related purposes, such as timekeeping, determining the time of the prayers in various geographical latitudes, using star positions for navigation, and determining the direction of the *qibla*.

Making astrolabes was then a crucial part of science in the Islamic era, and only a handful of skilled masters could make the most accurate and sophisticated ones. In his *Kitab al-Fihrist* ('A Book of Catalogue'), a compilation of the knowledge and literature of the tenth-century Muslim world, the famous Muslim biographer and scholar Ibn al-Nadīm (d. 998) lists the names of sixteen of the most accomplished and eminent makes of astrolabes and other machines in his time, when the Abbasids (751–1258) were at peak of their civilisational and scientific developments. Ibn al-Nadīm mentions a woman by the name of al-'Ijiliya (d. 967) towards the end of his list of these sixteen experts, claiming that she was amongst the pupils of Bitolus, a well-known tenth-century astrolabe maker who lived in Baghdad (Dodge, 1970, pp. 634–673). Recent researchers established her full name as being Maryam al-'Ijiliya al-Astrulabi. She was the daughter of the renowned astrolabe maker al-'Ijili al-Astrulabi, who had likewise received training by Bitolus to become a master in making the most innovative astrolabes of the time. Maryam al-'Ijiliya's hand-crafted astrolabe designs must have been quite intricate and inventive given that, from 944 to 967, alongside her father, she was employed at the court of Sayf al-Dawlah (r. 944–967), the founder of the Hamdanid dynasty in northern Syria (Jagot, 2023, p. 64). Except this, not much information is known about Maryam al-'Ijiliya's personal life, including whether or not she was ever married or had children. There is also no evidence of her birthplace or the precise location of her education in the art of instrument making.

In the field of mathematics, two names of Muslim female scholars who excelled in calculations and arithmetic are frequently cited. The first one is Sutayta al-Mahamali (d. 987), who was born in the Abbasid capital of Baghdad, the most advanced intellectual and scientific hub of that time, to a highly educated family. Her father, Abu 'Abdullah al-Hussain, was a judge (*qāḍī*) and authored several significant books on Islamic law (al-Baghdadi, 1931, vol. 6, p. 370). Her uncle was a *ḥadīth* expert and her son Abu-Hussain Muhammad bin Ahmad bin Ismail al-Mahamli was also a judge and was renowned for his just prosecution.

Sutayta excelled in many fields, including Arabic literature and grammar, *ḥadīth*, and *fiqh*, thanks to the intellectual and creative environment that prevailed in the capital of the Abbasid Empire in the tenth century and her birth into a scholarly family. But mathematics was the subject in which Sutayta truly excelled and was respected. She was recounted by later historians and scholars such as Ibn al-Khatib al-Baghdadi (d. 1071), Ibn al-Jawzī (d. 1201), and Ibn Kathīr (d. 1373) as an expert in *ḥisāb* (arithmetic) and *farā'iḍ* (inheritance calculations), both being practical branches of mathematics which were well developed in her time (al-Baghdadi, 1931, vol. 6, p. 370; al-Jawzi, 1940, vol. 14, pp. 161–202; Khalifa, 1941).

The subject of mathematics has always been a part of the curriculum at Islamic traditional educational institutions (*kuttābs* – primary schools, and *madrasahs* – high-level schools or colleges in the past that existed in the Islamic world). In Muslim communities, every single judge and even ordinary scholars were expected to be able to resolve jurisprudential issues related to inheritance, such as how to correctly distribute the property between people of varying relation to the deceased or how to calculate the annual proceeds from a business and an estate to pay various taxes such as *zakat* (a payment made annually on certain kinds of property of the wealthy stratum of Muslims, one of the Five Pillars of Islam) and *kharaj* (an individual tax on agricultural land and its harvest). Sutayta's abilities, however, extended well beyond these common questions of Islamic jurisprudence. She invented a number of equations and solutions that were cited by other mathematicians. While these equations were few in number, they demonstrate that her mathematical abilities extended beyond a basic aptitude for performing calculations.

Another well-known Muslim female who contributed to the discipline of mathematics was Labana (Lubna) (d. 984) of Cordoba in Muslim Spain. Originally born to a mother who had been a slave at the Madinah al-Zahra palace, she rose to prominence at the Umayyad Palace of Cordoba. She was well-versed in the exact sciences and was able to successfully solve even the most challenging geometrical and algebraic problems, according to Samuel Scott, a knowledgeable historian of Muslim rule in Spain. Due to Labana's extensive knowledge, the Caliph Al-Hakam II (r. 961–976) appointed her to the crucial position of private secretary (Scott, 1904, vol. 3, pp. 447–448). A biographical dictionary of scholars of Muslim Spain compiled by Ibn Bashkuwal (1101–1183), titled *Continuation of a Scholarly History of al-Andalūs* (*Kitāb al-Sila fī Ta'rīkh A'immat al-Andalūs*), describes her as 'an intelligent writer, grammarian, poetess, knowledgeable in mathematics and other sciences, and comprehensive in her learning. No one in the Umayyad palace was as noble and good as her' (Bashkuwal, 2008, vol. 2, p. 324).

Hakam II assembled a large library in the court of Cordoba with at least 400,000 manuscripts, which were imported at his request from all over the world and then duplicated by copywriters, among whom was Labana (Suzuki, 2009, p. 112). Her responsibility was not limited to duplicating books alone, as she also became entrusted with the care of the entire library. She studied accessible manuscripts, especially on exact sciences like the books of ancient Greek mathematicians Archimedes and Euclid, translated them, and wrote valuable commentaries and annotations on them.

Unfortunately, there is not much information available on Maryam, Labana, and Sutayta's personal lives or their scientific accomplishments outside of a few lines mentioning their names, expertise, and occupations in classical biographical dictionaries and history volumes. Yet even the very fact that their names are listed among those erudite giants of Islamic civilisation who utterly transformed the domain of science and technology with their discoveries, inventions, and concepts might be sufficient to realise the intellectual aptitude of these women who lived in the tenth century when the Islamic world was leading scientific and intellectual advancement. In addition, none of the manuscripts composed by them are known to us.

2.2 Muslim Women in the Medical Field and Healthcare

Throughout the Middle Ages (the fifth–fourteenth centuries CE), the knowledge of medicine was preserved and enriched by numerous innovative procedures, methods, and ideas in the Islamic world. When researching the history of Muslim Spain, Scott observed that 'The Arabs of Sicily, with their brethren of

Spain, owing to their extraordinary and thorough proficiency in medicine and surgery, were the most skillful practitioners in Europe' (Scott, 1904, p. 69).

Islam places a high value on maintaining one's physical and mental health, and personal hygiene. Thus, since the earliest period of Islam, Muslims developed the field of medicine by translating all the knowledge they had access to from Greek, Chinese, Persian, and Indian sources into Arabic and enhancing it with a substantial amount of innovative knowledge and novel techniques (Pormann & Savage-Smith, 2007, pp. 21–27).

In the beginning, the majority of physicians in the Muslim domains were Christians, but, starting from the ninth century, Muslims took the lead in the field of medicine as the most skilful practitioners and the authors of major compendiums on medicine and healthcare. For instance, towards the end of the ninth century, Muhammad Ibn Zakariyya Al-Razi (d. 925, Rhazes in Latin) emerged as a proponent of clinical medicine and observation, as well as a master of prognosis, psychosomatic medicine, and anatomy. Abu Ali Ibn Sina (d. 1037, Avicenna in Latin), one of the greatest minds of medieval Islam, whose multi-faceted studies encompassed such diverse scholarly fields as exegesis, law, logic, metaphysics, mathematics, astronomy, and medicine, was born in 980. His enormous medical encyclopaedia, entitled *Al-Qānūn fī al-Ṭibb* (The Canon of Medicine), was translated into Latin in ca. 1150 and subsequently became Europe's standard medical textbook until the seventeenth century and is still estimated as the most famous medical textbook ever produced (Akhmetova, 2018, pp. 108–111).

No substantial medical compendiums, textbooks, or even basic pamphlets were authored by women during the medieval Islamic period. Brilliant minds like Ibn Sina or Al-Razi who were capable of transforming the field of medicine with their innovative ideas, ground-breaking concepts, and discoveries did not emerge among Muslim women. Most of the historical sources and medical treatises are also silent about female patients and practitioners in the medieval Muslim world. Still, it would be too naïve to relate the absence of female scientists and authors in the medieval Islamic medical sciences and healthcare to the commonly accepted assumption that, up to modern times, the capacity of women was limited to the responsibility of 'midwives' alone. Nevertheless, in one capacity or another, Muslim women have frequently participated in medical practice and healthcare alongside men throughout Islamic history. In pre-Islamic Arabic poetry, women were depicted as being responsible for curing and treating wounded warriors (Ullmann, 1978, pp. 3–4; Pormann & Savage-Smith, 2007, pp. 103–105). With the advent of Islam, this tradition of women acting as healers continued in one way or another. There are numerous instances of Muslim women participating as nurses going back to the time of the Prophet

Muhammad. For instance, Islamic biographical collections (*sīrah* books) provide the names of nineteen women who participated in battles during the time of the Prophet, primarily as nurses who treated the sick and wounded (Roded, 1994, p. 35).

Among the earliest Muslim female physicians and nurses, Rufaidah bint Sa'ad from the Bani Aslam tribe in Madinah can be mentioned. She was among the first individuals in Madinah to embrace Islam during the lifetime of Muhammad. She would attend to the sick in a tent erected outside the Prophet's mosque in Madinah during times of peace. But during times of conflict, she would lead a team of volunteer nurses onto the battlefields to assist casualties on the front lines (Bsoul, 2018, p. 53). Together with her team, she participated in the battles of Badr (624), Uhud (625), Khandaq (627), and Khaibar (628). Her contribution during the battle of Khaibar was so valuable that Muhammad gave a share of the booty to Rufaidah in appreciation for her medical assistance that was equal portion to that of male soldiers who had participated in the war (Bsoul, 2018, p. 53). Biographical accounts describe Rufaidah as a well-respected woman who possessed the ideal qualities of a professional practitioner, including talent, compassion, empathy, good leadership, and the capacity to share her clinical expertise with colleagues and pupils (Al-Fanjari, 1980).

Another female companion of the Prophet Muhammad often cited in historical accounts for her therapeutic skills was al-Shifa (Layla) bint Abdullah (d. 640), who belonged to the 'Adi tribe of Quraysh (Siddiqi, 1982, p. 157). She rose to fame for developing a remedy that could prevent ant bites. It was narrated that, after the migration to Madinah in 622, al-Shifa approached the Prophet and said, 'O Messenger of Allah, I used to do preventative medicine for ant bites during Jahiliyya (literally, period of "ignorance", referring to the pre-Islamic period), and I want to demonstrate it for you'. The Prophet said, 'Demonstrate it'. Al-Shifa said, 'So I demonstrated it for him, and he said [continue to] do this, and teach it to Hafsah [the wife of the Prophet]' (Khan, 2007, p. 192).

Al-Tabari (839–923), in his historical chronicle titled *History of the Prophets and Kings*, mentioned that women used to heal infected wounds by making antiseptic creams. A few other medieval Islamic sources such as the *Kitāb al-Aghāni* (The Book of Songs) of the tenth-century historian Abu al-Faraj al-Isfahani (897–967) and the encyclopaedic work from the thirteenth century *'Uyūn Al-Anbā' fī Ṭabaqāt Al-Aṭibbā'* (Biographical Encyclopedia of Physicians) of Ibn Abi Usaibi'a (1203–1270) mentioned the name of Zainab Al-Awadiyya from the tribe of Banu Awd as a skilled physician and expert oculist in the seventh century Arabia, widely known for treating eye diseases and making specific topical drugs (Usaibi'a, 1998, p. 162). Ibn Abi Usaibi'a also mentioned two Andalusian female physicians from the al-Zuhar family, Umm 'Umar, who was the sister of Abu Bakr ibn Zuhar (d. 1194) and practised medicine along with her daughter. According to Bsoul, both of them specialised in obstetrics and gynaecology. They were the caliph's physicians to treat his wives and other members of the royal family (Bsoul, 2018, pp. 88–89).

Preservation of public healthcare is highly recommended in Islamic teachings and thus was considered one of the key responsibilities of the government. Henceforth, to provide healthcare for the general public, Muslim rulers began building mobile and permanent hospitals, known as *bimaristan* (*bimar-vīmār* or *vemār* – in Persian means 'sick' or 'ill person' while *stan* indicates a location) in various parts of the Muslim world as early as the eighth century. Muslim *bimaristans* had attained such outstanding levels of performance and quality by the twelfth and thirteenth centuries that travellers and historians deemed them to be one of the main achievements of Islamic civilisation. During the Seljuk (1037–1308) and Ottoman (1299–1922) dynasties, the number of hospitals and clinics, which were also called *bimarhane*, *darüşşifa* (house of healing), or *şifahane* (place of healing), multiplied and became an integral part of every *külliye*[2] (complex) erected under the patronage of the sultans, princes, or other members of the royal family. Remarkably, numerous *şifahanes* were constructed at the initiative, support, funding, and supervision of the female elite (Kılıç, 2015, p. 122).

These public healthcare institutions and *darüşşifa*s provided a proper setting for women to engage effectively in the field of professional healthcare, as male and female patient wards were divided in Muslim hospitals. The famous Ottoman explorer Evliya Çelebi (Derviş Mehmed Zilli, 1611–1682), for instance, visited the Fatih *darüşşifa* (constructed in 1470) in Istanbul in the seventeenth century and reported that it had a separate area that served as a hospital for women (Kilic, 2015, p. 209).

Islamic and cultural modesty norms favoured that the wards be staffed by people of the same gender as the patients. This practice quickly created both a need and an opportunity for skilled and highly qualified female medical professionals. Surty claims that 'the first official female nurses' (all from Sudan) were employed by al-Qayrawan (Kairouan) hospital, which was built in 830 by Prince Ziyadat Allah I of Ifriqiya (r. 817–838), the Aghlabid ruler

---

[2] A *külliye* is a large complex of buildings associated with the Turkish architecture that are centred on a mosque and are maintained by a single institution, often based on a *waqf* (charitable foundation). These complexes included educational facilities (*madrasah*), a hospital or clinic (*darulşifa*), a kitchen (*imarah*), a bakery, a guesthouse for travellers (*caravanserai*), a public bath (*hamam*), and other structures for various charitable services for the general public.

(Surty, 1996, p. 66). There is no information regarding whether these nurses had any training, were compensated financially, or what their specific responsibilities were. Historically, the term 'nurse' referred to someone who cared for the sick, without necessarily having received official training. The career of nursing in a modern sense only arose in the nineteenth century, becoming increasingly organised and secular.

Additionally, Ottoman sources such as *Cerrahiyyetu'l-Haniyye* (Imperial Surgery) by Şerefeddin Sabuncuoğlu (1385–1470) narrate the presence of skilled female doctors in the palaces (Bademci, 2006, p. 162). For instance, the *darüşşifa* (*Cariyeler Hastanesi*) at the Topkapı Palace, which provided care for the residents of the Ottoman administrative centre, had a female health team consisting of a female chief physician (*hekime kadın*), doctors called *hastalar ustası* (patients' master) and their assistants, and the female warden of patients (*hastalar kethüdası kadın*) and her assistant (*cariyesi*) (Sari, 2009; Sarı, 2021, pp. 199–200; Sarı & İzgöer, 2021, p. 222).

The employment of female doctors in the Ottoman palaces continued until the second half of the nineteenth century (Sari, 2021, pp. 199–200). One of the ten most proficient physicians working in Yıldız Palace in 1872 was Tabibe Gülbeyaz Kadın, a female doctor, with a monthly wage of 200 silver coins (Kılıç, 2015, pp. 288–293). Concerning the role of women in Ottoman medical research, the contemporary Turkish scholar in the history of medicine Nil Sarı informs us that female physicians called *morti tabibe* were employed at the quarantine office in Istanbul, probably for postmortem studies. In a document dated 1842, their salaries are listed in a register of wages of the quarantine personnel (Sari, 2009; Sarı, 2021, pp. 199–200).

There is at least one recorded case of a female head physician that occurred in seventeenth-century Ottoman Cairo in the Al-Mansuri *bimarstan*, the largest and earliest hospital in Egypt constructed in 1285. When the head physician Shihab Al-Din ibn Al-Sa'egh died in 1627, his daughter Binti Shihab Al-Din ibn Al-Sa'egh took over the position. The head physician was responsible for mentoring all other doctors in patient examination, disease diagnosis, and hospital administration (Al-Sa'eed, 1985).

An expert in Islamic studies and the transmission of the Greek medical and scientific heritage into the Islamic world, Peter Pormann emphasises that, even though the historical sources predominantly mention male physicians, several medieval medical treatises provide indications that women also provided important health services. These sources occasionally mention female physicians (*tabibah*), indicating that a few women from the families of famous physicians apparently had received an elite medical education (Pormann, 2009, pp. 1598–1599). Pre-modern Muslim communities featured both professionally trained female doctors and traditional female healers, including midwives, who were essential to healthcare and the preservation of cultural healing heritage. There is also some indirect proof in medical manuscripts, such as the testimony of certain male physicians who complain that their patients turn to 'women and the rabble' instead of consulting them (Pormann, 2009, pp. 1598–1599). Al-Zahrawi (936–1013), an eminent Andalusian surgeon and court physician to the Andalusian Umayyad caliph Al-Hakam II (r. 961–976), while explaining methods to extract bladder stones, commented that the procedure could be difficult for male doctors to perform on female patients due to the need to touch the genitalia. He therefore advised that a male practitioner should find a female doctor who is qualified to perform the procedure; otherwise, he can use a eunuch physician or a midwife who can follow instructions from a male surgeon (Green, 2003, vol. 1, pp. 358–361).

Nevertheless, the presence of female practitioners at Muslim hospitals in the past cannot simply be attributed to the necessity of female doctors to treat female patients. Scholars in Islamic jurisprudence touched on the issue although their opinions differ. For instance, Shams ad-Din al-Dhahabi (died ca. 1348) argued that in the case of disease, practitioners can treat the opposite sex, even if the patient has to expose their private parts. Pormann argues that al-Dhahabi's position was not exceptional among Muslim jurists, due to the legal maxim that *ḍarūrah* (necessity) outweighs other legal rules (Pormann, 2009, p. 1599). One of the leading Muslim scholars of the fifteenth century Jalal al-Din Abd al-Rahman al-Suyuti (1445–1505) in his treatise *al-Ṭibb al-Nabawī* (The Prophetic Medicine) also ruled that 'it is clearly halal (permitted) for a man to treat a woman to whom he is not related, and to see her private parts in cases of illness. And similarly, it is halal for a woman to treat a man, and to see his private parts in a case of illness, and if there is no man or woman from his family at hand' (as-Suyuti, 1994, p. 136). Nevertheless, the issues related to cross-gender interactions remain central in Islamic scholarship till the present (Ayubi, 2021; Zainuddin & Mahdy, 2017, pp. 353–360).

The Christian physician Sa'id ibn al-Hasan (d.1072) referred to the general role of women in Islamic societies as healers accordingly:

> How amazing is this [that patients are cured at all], considering that they hand over their lives to senile old women! For most people, at the onset of illness, use as their physicians either their wives, mothers or aunts, or some [other] member of their family or one of their neighbours. He [the patient] acquiesces to whatever extravagant measure she might order, consumes whatever she prepares for him, and listens to what she says and obeys her commands more than he obeys the physician. (Pormann, 2009, p. 1599)

In this way, women likely provided medical care for people of both sexes in their societies. Yet, as our discussion disclosed, women in Islamic history were not engaged in the medical field as trained physicians; rather, they mostly served as uneducated practitioners. At the same time, there were also cases of qualified Muslim women who had been employed as physicians or even as surgeons. Şerefeddin Sabuncuoğlu (1385–1470), a Turkish Ottoman surgeon and qualified medical scientist who worked at the most advanced hospitals of his time in Amasya, illustrated the details of obstetric and gynaecologic procedures in his comprehensive manual on surgery, *Cerrahiyyetu'l-Haniyye* (Imperial Surgery) in the form of miniatures. Some miniatures in *Cerrahiyyetu'l-Haniyye* depict female surgeons, acknowledged by Sabuncuoğlu as *tabibe*, at the surgical process of managing a dead foetus with foetal hydrocephalus and microcephalus (Figure 1). Bademci described these miniatures as the first clues of Turkish Muslim women carrying out paediatric neurosurgery in the fifteenth century (Bademci, 2006, p. 162). Female surgeons of fifteenth-century Anatolia are reported to be skilled in performing various gynaecological procedures such as surgical management of the fleshy growth of the clitoris, imperforated female pudenda, warts, and red pustules arising in the female pudenda, perforations and eruptions of the uterus, abnormal labours, and extractions of the abnormal foetus or placenta.

Figure 1 A Miniature in Şerefeddin Sabuncuoğlu's *Cerrahiyyetu'l-Haniyye* which depicts Adult Hermaphroditism Conducted by a Female Doctor
Source: (Korkmaz, 2021)

There are records of Muslim women practising medicine and healing in Europe as well. Muslim and Jewish women practised medicine prior to the forced conversion of Muslims to Catholicism through a series of edicts outlawing Islam in the Spanish Monarchy between 1500 and 1526. They were held in high regard, and both male and female physicians treated members of the Spanish upper class, including King Philip II (r. 1556–1598). In 1329, Alfonso IV of Valencia (r. 1327–1336) introduced strict regulations regarding Christian women, ruling that 'no woman may practice medicine or give potions, under penalty of being whipped through town' although they were permitted 'to care for little children, and women – to whom, however, they may give no potion' (Whaley, 2011, p. 36). In 1346, the Black Death started in Spain and, due to the shortage of physicians, women, Muslim, and Jewish physicians were allowed to lawfully practise medicine. In Spanish hospitals, Muslim women, known as *metgesses*, worked as midwives, doctors, and surgeons for both the Muslim and Christian communities. Their work went beyond nursing, as one record indicates bone-setting a fracture, and for which they were paid. Commonly, Muslim women practitioners practised midwifery, surgery, and general medicine, including one of them, Cahud, who worked as a doctor in the royal household of Valencia. Muslim women were permitted to sit for an examination set by licensed surgeons and, if they passed, were permitted to practise.

In sum, Muslim women participated in various types of medical care, from nursing and providing first aid to ophthalmology, surgery, general therapy, and midwifery, including supervision and institutional management.

3 Contemporary Muslim Women in Sciences

As of 2011, there are forty-nine Muslim-majority states situated in the Asian, European, and African continents. These countries are home to 1.2 billion Muslims; or 74 per cent of the 1.6 billion Muslims worldwide. Except for Albania and Kosovo, which are in Europe, all nations with Muslim-majority populations are in less developed regions of the world.[3] In addition, almost one-fourth of the global Muslim population live as minorities in non-Muslim countries such as India, China, Russia, and the United States, as well as in Africa and Europe. In thirty countries, Muslims make up the second-largest group. In many African countries, especially those that make up the sub-Saharan belt, Islam is the second most popular religion after Christianity.[4]

---

[3] PEW Research Center. (2011). *Muslim-Majority Countries*, www.pewresearch.org/religion/ 2011/01/27/future-of-the-global-muslim-population-muslim-majority.

[4] Hackett, C. & Huynh, T. (2015). *What Is Each Country's Second-Largest Religious Group*, www .pewresearch.org/short-reads/2015/06/22/what-is-each-countrys-second-largest-religious-group.

Hence, when we discuss contemporary Muslim female scientists, we are referring to a vast region and diverse communities with distinct cultural, geographical, political, and economic peculiarities although they all practice Islam. This study observes the contributions of Muslim women to contemporary scientific advancements and inventions in five Muslim-majority nations: Pakistan, Malaysia, Turkey, Qatar, and Jordan.

Each selected country has distinctive characteristics. Pakistan is one of the Muslim nations with the lowest gender parity in educational attainment, employment, and economic participation (36.2%) after Yemen, and the lowest female literacy rate worldwide after Afghanistan.[5] Furthermore, Pakistan is considered in this study as a representative of the entire South Asian region with a significant Muslim population (640 million Muslims in Pakistan, Bangladesh, India, Sri Lanka, Nepal, and Bhutan combined). Malaysia, on the other hand, is a representative case for Southeast Asia. Turkey, which has never been under colonial domination, represents the regions of Europe, Central Asia, and the Black Sea. It is the best example of how Mustafa Kemal Atatürk's (1881–1938) policies based on westernisation, modernisation, and secularisation empowered Muslim women at the start of the twentieth century. As a result, Turkey began implementing strict laws that aimed at empowering women a century ago as between 1920 and 1938, 10 per cent of all university graduates in Turkey were women. Qatar is a young and oil-rich country that emerged in 1971. There are just 811,600 women in Qatar, which is less than one-third of the country's total population (compared to 2,034,518 men). Qatar is also a unique nation in which female literacy rates are higher than male literacy rates. A Muslim Arab nation in the Middle East, Jordan boasts both political and economic stability. Its history as a hub for great civilisations including the Assyrian, Babylonian, Roman, Byzantine, and Islamic is extensive. In both schools and universities, there is an unprecedented level of gender balance in Jordan.

Each country report begins with a summary of the female literacy rate, the level of gender parity, and women's involvement in the STEM sectors. Nevertheless, it would be unfair to generalise about the role of contemporary Muslim women in the STEM sectors of the entire world based on these isolated five cases. We firmly believe that every region or country has its own unique experience, traditions, advantages, and realities. These five examples are provided just to highlight the diversity, depth, and distinctions within the Muslim world.

---

[5] World Economic Forum. (2023). *Global Gender Gap Report 2023*, www.weforum.org/reports/global-gender-gap-report-2023/in-full/benchmarking-gender-gaps-2023.

3.1 Pakistan

The Constitution of Pakistan (Article 25-A under the 18th Amendment) obligates the state to offer free and compulsory education to children up to the secondary level between the ages of five and sixteen, although its implementation has never been fully enforced. Both boys and girls are missing out on education in intolerable numbers, but girls are worst affected.

At the 2015 Oslo Summit on Education and Development, Pakistan was listed as 'among the worst performing countries in education'. According to the manifesto of the Pakistani government from July 2018, there are over 22.5 million children who are not in school, with girls being disproportionately affected. Table 1 shows that in Pakistan, at the age of obligatory education, 56 per cent of girls and 44 per cent of boys do not attend school. More precisely, 32 per cent of girls in primary school are not enrolled, compared to 21 per cent of boys. By grade six, 59 per cent of girls and 49 per cent of boys are out of school. By the ninth grade, only 13 per cent of girls are still enrolled (Human Rights Watch, 2018, p. 2).[6]

Low female enrolment in education in Pakistan, especially in rural areas, is commonly explained by the state's ineffective funding of schools, corruption, insecurity and violence, customs, early marriage, gender-based discrimination, harassment, poverty, and families' inability to pay for their children to attend schools (Human Rights Watch, 2018, pp. 74–84).

The exceptionally low literacy rate among Pakistani women produces a huge gender gap in STEM fields. For instance, only 4.9 per cent of engineering jobs are occupied by women in Pakistan while only 3 per cent of engineers in the

Table 1 Gender-based comparison of children not enrolled in schools in Pakistan

Level	Percentage of Girls Not Enrolled in Schools	Percentage of Boys Not Enrolled in Schools
Primary school	32%	21%
Secondary school (grade 6)	59%	49%
Grade 9	87%	No data
General	56%	44%

Source: Human Rights Watch (2018)

---

[6] Abbasi. (2021). *Girls Education in Pakistan: A Holistic Analysis*, https://baat.kfueit.edu.pk/girls-education-in-pakistan-a-holistic-analysis.

energy sector are women.[7] Despite this, there are many accomplished female scientists in Pakistan who have gained recognition on an international level for their discoveries and significant contributions to the advancement of science and technology.

3.2 Malaysia

Malaysia, a Southeast Asian nation with a Muslim majority population, has a reverse gender gap in higher education: girls outnumber boys at universities and have achieved an impressive level of gender parity in the STEM sectors (Tienxhi, 2017, p. 1). Malaysia's population comprises many ethnic groups, but most of the population is of Austronesian descent (67.4%), who are indigenous to the Malay Peninsula and are referred to as the Bumiputras. There are also sizable populations of Chinese (24.6%) and Indians (7.3%), who are descended from those who migrated to the region during British colonial administration.

Since its independence from the British in 1957, Malaysia has undergone a series of substantial educational reforms, particularly aiming at increasing female participation in education. According to Malaysia's Gender Gap Index report, the combined gross enrolment ratio was in favour of men in 1980 (53%–56.9%), but parity was attained by 1990; women have had a higher enrolment ratio since 2000 (65.3%–64.3%) (Ministry of Women, Family and Community Development Malaysia, 2007).

Malaysia hence experiences the opposite of what occurs in Pakistan. Table 2 demonstrates the existing gender disparity in higher education enrolment in Malaysia.

As Table 2 displays, in seven of the eight major fields of study, including those where women have historically been underrepresented, like mathematics and science, women outnumber men in Malaysia. The only fields in which men continue to outnumber women are engineering, manufacturing, and construction. In 2018, the ratio of male students to female students in Malaysian public universities was 1:1.6 (38.08% male to 61.92% female) (Ministry of Education Malaysia, 2018, p. 35).

In comparison to other countries in the East Asia and Pacific area, Malaysia's high proportion of female students in higher education is unique. While women make up 67 per cent of students in the social sciences, business, and law in Malaysia, the regional average for female representation in the same field of study is below 50 per cent. In the region, female students are underrepresented in the fields of science and mathematics. In Malaysia, however, women make up

---

[7] Ahmed, A. (2018). *Pakistan among Worst Performers on Gender Equality: WEF*, www.dawn.com/news/1452284.

Table 2 Enrolment and graduation data at Public Universities in Malaysia (as of December 2017)

Fields of Study	Enrolment (Male)	Enrolment (Female)	Graduate (Male)	Graduate (Female)
Education	9,994	25,420	2,304	6,381
Arts and Humanities	18,484	33,472	3,513	6,720
Social Sciences, Business, and Law	54,927	119,406	12,017	28,694
Science, Mathematics, and Computer	30,229	54,043	6,264	13,866
Engineering, Manufacturing, and Construction	69,204	57,959	14,008	12,698
Agriculture and Veterinary	5,076	7,427	933	1,454
Health and Welfare	9,087	24,552	1,747	5,056
Services	7,915	10,893	1,626	2,277

Source: Ministry of Education Malaysia (2018, p. 34)

62.8 per cent of the student population in these subjects. Women in Malaysia are still a minority in the fields of engineering, manufacturing, and construction, although they are far closer to gender parity compared to the regional average, which is less than 20 per cent compared to 43.1 per cent in Malaysia (Tienxhi, 2017, p. 8).

Such outstanding representation of women in Malaysian universities can be the result of state policies to increase girls' participation in STEM education and research. The Malaysian government has placed STEM education as a focal point in the process of becoming a developed nation. It acknowledges the importance of women and has formulated policies such as the Malaysian Woman Policy from 2009 and the National Policy on Science, Technology, and Innovation from 2013 to 2020. These policies have increased women researchers in STEM from 35.8 per cent in 2004 to 49.9 per cent in 2012.[8]

Nevertheless, as UNESCO's Institute for Statistics 2015 report emphasises, there is a 'tendency for female participation to decrease as the level of education rises'.[9] The percentage of Malaysian women in STEM fields declines sharply at the highest levels of both education and employment (see Table 3).

---

[8] Pittman, Taylor. (2019). *10 Facts About Girls' Education in Malaysia – The Borgen Project*, https://borgenproject.org/10-facts-about-girls-education-in-malaysia.

[9] UNESCO. (2015). *A Complex Formula: Girls and Women in Science, Technology, Engineering and Mathematics in Asia*, http://unesdoc.unesco.org/images/0024/002457/245717E.pdf.

Table 3 Percentage of women in STEM education (Malaysian Public Universities)

Degree	Level	Men	Women	Total	GPI[a]	% of Women
Engineering	Bachelors	42309	34615	76924	0.82	45
	Masters	6543	6377	12920	0.97	49
	Doctorate	4380	2607	6987	0.6	37
Mathematics	Bachelors	1512	4450	5962	2.94	75
	Masters	264	709	973	2.69	73
	Doctorate	313	369	682	1.18	54
Science	Bachelors	3286	8275	11561	2.52	72
	Masters	3909	7121	11030	1.82	65
	Doctorate	2102	2506	4608	1.19	54
Technology	Bachelors	2581	4098	6679	1.59	61
	Masters	534	540	1074	1.01	50
	Doctorate	333	180	513	0.54	35

[a] The Global Parity Index (GPI) is a measure to capture the changing gender demographics of university enrolment. A GPI of less than 1 represents a disparity in favour of males, while a GPI above 1 represents a disparity in favour of females.
Source: Malaysian Higher Education Statistics (Tienxhi, 2017, p. 11)

Table 3 shows that, with the exception of engineering, women have surpassed men in the STEM areas at the BA and MA degree levels in Malaysia, although their percentage declines as education level advances. Women continue to dominate in the fields of science and mathematics even at the doctoral level. Although there is a significant decline in the proportion of female postgraduate students and researchers, Malaysia has nonetheless achieved an impressive level of gender parity in the STEM fields when compared to the global underrepresentation of women in these professions. For instance, according to the UNESCO Institute for Statistics (UIS), in 2015, just 28 per cent of scientists and researchers globally were women.[10]

3.3 Turkey

In the past few years, Turkey has experienced a 40 per cent growth in the proportion of female students majoring in STEM subjects.[11] According to the Eurostat statement released on 11 February 2019 to mark the International Day

---

[10] UNESCO. (2015). *A Complex Formula: Girls and Women in Science, Technology, Engineering and Mathematics in Asia*, http://unesdoc.unesco.org/images/0024/002457/245717E.pdf.
[11] Hürriyet. (2021). *Turkish Women Scientists' Ratio Surpasses EU Average, Data Shows*, www.hurriyetdailynews.com/turkish-women-scientists-ratio-surpasses-eu-average-data-shows-162600.

of Women and Girls in Science, Turkey has a higher percentage of women scientists and engineers than the EU average. The EU average of women scientists and engineers is 41 per cent, while it is 45 per cent in Turkey. In comparison to several developed EU nations like Germany, France, the UK, and Italy, Turkey has a larger proportion of female scientists and engineers.[12]

Hasan Mandal, the chairman of the Scientific and Technological Research Council of Turkey (TÜBİTAK), also noted that 58 per cent of researchers who were funded by TÜBİTAK's programmes for scientists in 2020 were women.[13] The active participation of female scientists in the advancement of science and technology, and innovative developments in Turkey is a consequence of the government's policies, particularly the efforts of TÜBİTAK to maintain a balance between male and female researchers at all levels of activities.

One of TÜBİTAK's core policy tenets is to embrace a gender balance for the participation of female and male researchers while giving priority to increasing the ratio of female researchers in such a way as to achieve balance in decision-making processes, such as group executive boards and advisory boards, and project evaluation and monitoring processes while ensuring scientific excellence and/or research quality. The TÜBİTAK Women in Science Award, which is granted to female scientists who have made noteworthy contributions to science and technology in Turkey, is one of the projects run by TÜBİTAK to encourage women to pursue careers in science and technology.[14]

The active participation of Turkish women in scientific developments and scholarship is not a new phenomenon. Some elite women during the Seljuk and Ottoman dynasties participated in educational and scholarly developments, public healthcare, and the welfare of their societies. Adjacent to the Tanzimat educational reforms between 1839 and 1876, modern-style universities began to appear in the Ottoman lands, and, in 1914, the first women's university, the *Inas Dar'ül Fünun*, opened in Istanbul for female students who passed the entrance exam following the high schools. In 1917, the government allowed women to enrol in medical, pharmaceutical, and chemistry programmes (Gelişli, 2004, pp. 125–126). Halide Edib (1884–1964) was the first Turkish woman to lecture at Istanbul University (then known as *Darülfunun*) in 1918.

---

[12] Mehmet, F. H. (2019). *Turkish Women Scientists' Ratio Surpasses EU Average*, www.aa.com.tr/en/europe/turkish-women-scientists-ratio-surpasses-eu-average/1390691.

[13] Hürriyet. (2021). *Turkish Women Scientists' Ratio Surpasses EU Average, Data Shows*, www.hurriyetdailynews.com/turkish-women-scientists-ratio-surpasses-eu-average-data-shows-162600.

[14] TÜBİTAK. (2020). *Policy Principles for Increasing the Participation of Women Researchers in TÜBİTAK Processes Are Published*, www.tubitak.gov.tr/en/news/policy-principles-for-increasing-the-participation-of-women-researchers-in-tubitak-processes-are.

After the establishment of the Turkish Republic in 1923, Atatürk's social and educational reforms aimed to expand women's public roles. Turkey is regarded as the country that best exemplified the empowerment of Muslim women at the dawn of the twentieth century through westernisation, modernisation, and secularisation. The primary goal of Atatürk's reforms was to alter the traditional status of women in society because modernisation and westernisation were viewed as the only paths to achieving women's empowerment. Republican women were urged to pursue higher education, earn professional degrees, and contribute to the development of the nation. Already between 1920 and 1938, 10 per cent of all university graduates in Turkey were women. In 1935, eighteen women were elected to the Turkish Parliament that had around 400 members in total (White, 2003, pp. 150–151).

Several women appeared as the ideal of a modernised Turkish woman during the early decades of the Republic. One of them was Sabiha Gökçen (1913–2001), a Turkish pilot who was Atatürk's adopted daughter. The Guinness Book of World Records recognises Gökçen as being the world's first female fighter pilot. She flew for a total of about 8,000 hours throughout her career, taking part in thirty-two military operations, and in 1938, she spent five days on a historic peace mission around the Balkans.[15]

According to the American Professor in Turkish Studies Jenny White, the radical reforms that intended to create modern Turkish republican women during the early Republican period focused primarily on urban women who made up just 20 per cent of the country's female population. A vast majority of women (80%) still lived in rural areas and were left behind (White, 2003, p. 147). In contemporary Turkey, there is still a problem with girls' education in rural areas, particularly in the southeastern provinces of Bitlis, Van, and Hakkari. Two-thirds of Turkey's more than five million illiterate adults are women as of 2015, with rural women making up the majority of this group. Over the past few decades, Turkey has made impressive progress towards ensuring that everyone has access to education. In 2006, 91 per cent of children aged six to fifteen attended elementary school, while the total literacy rate for male and female adults was 90 per cent and 70 per cent, respectively (Hanemann, 2015, p. 89).

The World Bank estimates that women make up only 32.7 per cent of Turkey's labour force in 2022.[16] Despite their low participation in the labour sectors in general, women in Turkey are quite well represented in the business

---

[15] Ergil, L. Y. (2021). *Women's History Month: Celebrating the Courageous Women of Turkey*, www.dailysabah.com/turkey/expat-corner/womens-history-month-celebrating-the-courageous-women-of-turkey.

[16] World Bank. (2022). *Labor Force, Female (% of Total Labor Force)*, https://data.worldbank.org/indicator/SL.TLF.TOTL.FE.ZS.

world and academia. For instance, a Thomson-Reuters survey found that the percentage of female academicians in Turkey is 47.5 per cent which is one of the highest in the world.[17] Turkish women are actively engaged in the STEM fields both nationally and internationally as scientists, engineers, developers, and specialists.

3.4 Qatar

With 2.8 million people (as of Qatar Census 2020), Qatar is a small peninsular Arab nation in Western Asia. Qatar is regarded as one of the more recent states as it only obtained its independence from the British in 1971. All citizens are entitled to free public education, and six years of primary school attendance is required for all children. The policy of compulsory education led to an increase in literacy from 74 per cent in 1985 to 81 per cent in 2000.

Qatar is a unique nation in which female literacy rates are higher than male literacy rates. As of 2017, 94.71 per cent of all women and 93.14 per cent of men over the age of fifteen years were literate, that is, able to read and write (see Table 4).

With separate faculties for men and women, Qatar University was founded as the country's first university in 1973. By 2012, the number of female students became roughly twice the number of male students. Women in Qatar have also advanced significantly in STEM-related sectors that were previously considered to be male-dominated career paths. For instance, Texas A&M University in

Table 4 Adult Literacy Rate in Qatar between 2012 and 2017

Year	Adult Literacy Rate (female)	Adult Literacy Rate (male)	Adult Literacy Rate (total)
2017	94.71%	93.14%	93.46%
2016	94.21%	92.88%	93.15%
2014	92.45%	91.05%	91.33%
2013	91.73%	90.34%	90.63%
2012	90.81%	90.00%	90.17%

Source: Country Economy (https://countryeconomy.com/demography/literacy-rate/qatar)[18]

---

[17] Bora, B. (2013). *Türk Akademisi Cinsiyet Eşitliğinde Birinci* [A Turkish Academia Is First in Gender Parity], www.hurriyet.com.tr/gundem/turk-akademisi-cinsiyet-esitliginde-birinci-23209818.

[18] *Qatar – Literacy Rate*, https://countryeconomy.com/demography/literacy-rate/qatar.

Qatar, which offers degrees in chemical, electrical, mechanical, and petroleum engineering, had about 40 per cent female students in 2015.[19]

Science and women's empowerment are both considered essential for the achievement of internationally agreed development goals, including the 2030 Sustainable Development Agenda, of which Qatar is a part (Naguib & Aref, 2024, p. 75). Qatar has created a number of initiatives to encourage women in science in order to attain gender equality in STEM, such as the Qatar National Research Fund, which awards money to female-led research projects.[20] In 2018, the UNESCO Institute for Statistics reported that 34.1 per cent of Qatar's researchers were female. This is slightly higher than the 33.3 per cent global average.[21] Moreover, given the fact that women only make up barely one-third of Qatar's total population (811,600 females to 2,034,518 males;[22] see Figure 2), the active involvement of Qatari women in research is astounding.

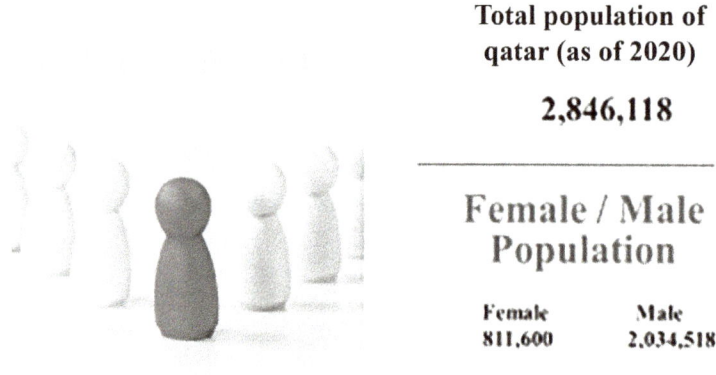

Figure 2 The population of Qatar in 2020
Source: National Planning Council (2020)[23]

---

[19] Qazi, S. (2015). *In Qatar, Education Drives Workforce Shifts for Women*, www.al-fanarmedia.org/2015/08/in-qatar-education-drives-workforce-shifts-for-women/.
[20] Saleem, F. (2023). *Women in Qatar Strive in Science*, https://m.thepeninsulaqatar.com/article/11/02/2023/women-in-qatar-strive-in-science.
[21] UNESCO Science Report. (2021). *Share of Women among Total Researchers by Country, 1996–2018*, www.unesco.org/reports/science/2021/en/dataviz/share-women-researchers-radial.
[22] The significant gender imbalance is primarily due to the substantial influx of male migrant workers from nations such as India, Pakistan, and Nepal, who arrive in Qatar seeking employment opportunities, frequently leaving their families in their home countries. A mere 11.6% of Qatar's populace comprises citizens, whereas expatriates and migrant workers constitute the overwhelming majority, accounting for approximately 88.4% of the total demographic landscape.
[23] National Planning Council. (2020). *Qatar Census 2020*, www.psa.gov.qa/en/statistics1/StatisticsSite/Census/census2020/results/Pages/default.aspx.

3.5 Jordan

The Hashemite Kingdom of Jordan stands at the intersection of Asia, Africa, and Europe. In comparison to other neighbouring Middle Eastern states in the Levant region, it currently enjoys national security and stability and has a rich history as one of the centres of great civilisations, including the Assyrian, Babylonian, Roman, Byzantine, and Islamic.

In Jordan, ten years of basic education and two years of secondary academic or vocational education are compulsory. The literacy rate in Jordan for adults over fifteen was 98.42 per cent in 2021, according to the data provider Statista.[24] This is the highest number in the Middle East and the Arab world. Particularly among Jordanian women over the age of fifteen, there has been a remarkable increase in literacy. In 2007, the female literacy rate was 88.9 per cent; in the next fourteen years, it increased to 98.13 per cent by 2021. As a result, by 2021, the gender gap in literacy has significantly shrunk (male: 98.71%; female: 98.13%).[25]

Jordan has achieved gender parity in elementary school attendance since 1980, and women are enrolling in secondary and tertiary education at higher rates than males. If we consider that literacy among Jordanian female adults (15 years old and above) was only 15.2 per cent in 1970 compared to 50.1 per cent among male adults, this is a noteworthy success in female education (Youssef, 1976–1977, p. 193). The reverse gender gap in Jordan is a tendency that is present in other Arab nations. For instance, in science, three of the six Arab nations that took part in the Programme for International Student Assessment (PISA) 2015 were in the top five worldwide for reverse gender gaps: Jordan was placed first, the UAE second, and Qatar was fourth.[26]

According to the PISA 2018 report, Jordanian students' performance in mathematics and science is below the global average, although girls perform better. In 2015, Jordan also had the second-biggest reverse gender gap in mathematics (14 points) and the largest reverse gender gap in science (equal to more than a year of study). In mathematics, fifteen-year-olds earn 400 points, compared to an OECD average of 489 points. Girls outperform boys by a significant 6-point

---

[24] Statista. (2023). *Jordan: Literacy Rate from 2007 to 2018, Total and by Gender*, www.statista.com/statistics/572748/literacy-rate-in-jordan/#:~:text=Jan%2025%2C%202023%20The%20statistic%20depicts%20the%20literacy,2021%2C%20Jordan%27s%20literacy%20rate%20was%20around%2098.42%20percent.

[25] Statista. (2024). *Jordan: Literacy rate from 2007 to 2021, total and by gender*, www.statista.com/statistics/572748/literacy-rate-in-jordan/#:~:text=Jan%2025%2C%202023%20The%20statistic%20depicts%20the%20literacy,2021%2C%20Jordan%27s%20literacy%20rate%20was%20around%2098.42%20percent.

[26] OECD. (2015). *Program for International Student Assessment (PISA) School and Student Survey Dataset*, www.oecd.org/pisa/data.

margin (OECD average: boys outperform girls by 5 points). On the other hand, the average science performance among the same-age Jordanian pupils is 429 points, as opposed to an average of 489 points in OECD nations. With a statistically significant difference of 29 points, girls once again outperform boys (OECD average: 2 points higher for girls).[27] Hence, at the university level, more than 60 per cent of Jordanian students majoring in the natural sciences, medicine, dentistry, and pharmacy are female; the percentages for engineering and computer science are respectively approximately 28 per cent and 45 per cent.[28] In Jordanian schools and colleges, accordingly, girls perform better than boys, but this does not translate into a rise in the number of female researchers in higher-level STEM fields. Men still dominate the STEM research landscape in Jordan, and significant gender disparities in research can be observed. According to the UNESCO Science Report (UNESCO, 2015), women made up 26 per cent of researchers in the natural sciences, 18 per cent in engineering, 44 per cent in the medical sciences, 19 per cent in the agricultural sciences, and 32 per cent in the social sciences and humanities in 2008. According to the UNESCO Institute for Statistics, between 2008 and 2015, the proportion of women researchers fell from 22.5 per cent to 19.7 per cent.[29]

With the above brief review, we must keep in mind that every Muslim nation state is distinct with its own idiosyncratic ethnic and cultural diversity, traditions, historical realities, social and economic provisions, national priorities, and long-standing concerns (Rizzo et al., 2007, p. 1155). Therefore, the Muslim world varies widely in terms of education, gender gap, and job security.

4 Muslim Women and Science-Related Issues

This section explores a few issues that are central to comprehending Muslim women's contributions to scientific and technological developments in the past and present. Its first point deliberates the reasons that have contributed to a decline in women's involvement in knowledge production and scientific advancements in Muslim societies since the twelfth century. It draws attention to the correlation between the deterioration of women's status and their engagement in scholarship and the public sphere, and a general decline of scientific productivity in Muslim societies.

---

[27] OECD. (2015). *Program for International Student Assessment (PISA) School and Student Survey Dataset*, www.oecd.org/pisa/data.

[28] UNESCO. (2022). *Jordanian Women Shine in Science*, www.unesco.org/en/articles/jordanian-women-shine-science.

[29] UNESCO Institute for Statistics. (2023). *Science, Technology and Innovation: Researchers by Sex, per Million Inhabitants, per Thousand Labour Force, per Thousand Total Employment (FTE and HC)*, http://data.uis.unesco.org/index.aspx?queryid=64.

The discussion evolves further into issues related to historiography. One significant challenge to studying women in Muslim societies in the early period of Islam is finding primary sources. Besides, those who recorded historical happenings were mostly unconcerned about ordinary women, except the most influential women due to their family's nobility and social ranking. However, as the conversation goes further, it becomes clear that an inadequate engagement of women in science and scholarship in medieval and pre-modern societies (prior to the mid-eighteenth century) was not an issue that affected Muslims alone. Different cultures and societies have different justifications for treating women unfairly.

The last two issues, on the other hand, concentrate on the factors that contribute to the limitations in knowledge production in the Muslim world, such as insufficient educational training and intellectual development of Muslim youth at early levels of education, and the underrepresentation of Muslim women in STEM-related academia and research.

4.1 Women and Scientific Productivity Decline in the Muslim World

Women's contributions to the advancement of science in pre-modern Muslim societies were limited, as the previous section of the Element demonstrated. In essence, there is no religious prohibition against women participating in science and scholarship (Sonbol, 2003, p. 6). However, in pre-modern Muslim communities, due to safety concerns and local customs, it was not always possible for women to acquire knowledge alongside men. In the early centuries of Islam, women's education was not a problem, and several women became leading educators and scholars. Throughout centuries, the number of women who were engaged in science, scholarship, and even public welfare became fewer and fewer (Majid, 1998, p. 323; Charrad, 2011, p. 428).

According to John Esposito, the freedom and equality enjoyed by women in the early centuries were replaced by their subjugated position in later Arab society: 'Many historical events such as the Mongol and Turkish invasions and the subsequent decline of the Muslim civilisation into feudalism were general causes for the deterioration of women's status' (Esposito, 1975, pp. 106–107). As Lebanese anthropologist and historian Nejla Izzeddin observes: 'When Arab society was productive, creative women participated in its activities and shared in the general strength and well-being. When vitality ebbed away and deterioration set in, a woman suffered along with her community' (Esposito, 1975, p. 107).

Between the ninth and as far as the sixteenth century, the Islamic world experienced an age of scientific discoveries and advancements. The Abbasid caliphate (751–1258) oversaw the most productive intellectual and scientific movement in the Islamic world and was the greatest power of that time until it fell prey to the Mongol invasion in 1258. Available scientific works of the classical Greeks, Chinese, and Indians were translated into Arabic. In addition to their translations of classical scientific treatises and writing commentaries on them, Muslim scholars also made original contributions through writing and meticulous experimentation in a variety of subjects, including philosophy, astronomy, medicine, chemistry, geography, physics, optics, and mathematics (Ofek, 2011).

Political scientist Hillel Ofek attributes the development of intellectual and scientific culture in Islamic civilisation to the material backdrop that came with the emergence of a strong and affluent empire. Scientific activity reached its peak when Islam was the dominant civilisation in the world. Yet, he suggests, the Muslim dynasties that emerged after the Mongol invasion or even late-Abbasid society were not able to maintain the previously experienced public ingenuity and culture that was hospitable to scientific advancement, although some practical innovations continued to emerge in various politically significant centres of Muslim domain (Ofek, 2011). Although these Muslim states were politically and economically strong, scientific productivity became constrained and never reached the levels previously observed during the Abbasids and the Umayyad rule in Andalusia. After the fourteenth century, the Muslim world experienced fewer and fewer advancements in fields that it had previously dominated, such as medicine, chemistry, or optics. The scholarship became excessively theologically and politically oriented. Madrasah curricula also began gradually losing an emphasis on science-related courses. All these changes resulted in a gradual decrease in scientific productivity and initiatives throughout the Muslim world. Simultaneously, a 'dependency on foreign scientific discoveries, institutions, and technology began to take hold' (Saliba, 2007, p. 247) in the Muslim world, which is referred to by Asadullah Ali Al-Andalusi, the founder of the Andalusian Project, an independent research platform on Islamic studies and related global issues, as the 'age of dependency' (Al-Andalusi, 2015, p. 241).

There is no simple explanation for the continuous decline in scientific inspiration and productivity in the Muslim world. The reduction in intellectual creativity was undoubtedly influenced by physical and geopolitical reasons, particularly in light of the rapidly expanding colonial and industrial powers of Europe since the fifteenth century.

Ofek attributes the decline of science in the Muslim world to the ascendance of the Ash'ari school to prominence as a major theological school and their growing opposition to original research and any scientific investigation that did not directly support religious control over private and public life

(Ofek, 2011). Toby Huff, chancellor professor of sociology at the University of Massachusetts, Dartmouth, also argued that in order to preserve intellectual originality and ingenuity in any community, people must be free from the censure of political and religious authorities:

> If in the long run scientific thought and intellectual creativity in general are to keep themselves alive and advance into new domains of conquest and creativity, multiple spheres of freedom – what we may call neutral zones – must exist within which large groups of people can pursue genius free from the censure of political and religious authorities. In addition, certain metaphysical and philosophical assumptions must accompany this freedom. Insofar as science is concerned, individuals must be conceived as being endowed with reason, the world may be thought to be a rational and consistent whole, and various levels of universal representation, participation, and discourse must be available. It is precisely here that one finds the great weaknesses of Arabic-Islamic civilization as an incubator of modern science. (Huff, 2003, p. 219)

It is true that Islamic theology became institutionalised over the course of centuries in Muslim history due to certain dynasties' preferences for a particular school of thought and the development of religious authorities. Still, the European experience with the Church may not explain the scientific decline in Islamic civilisation entirely as there was no such serious 'conflict between religion and science' as did happen in Europe due to the difference in culture and ideology (Al-Andalusi, 2015, p. 239).

Nevertheless, in this Element, we are interested in drawing attention to the connections between a general decline in scientific ingenuity and the rights of women to participate in public and scholarly activities. Interestingly, Asma Afsaruddin refutes the idea that women's roles in the public sphere, whether they are characterised politically, culturally, economically, or, in terms of religious scholarship and leadership, experienced a decline after the third/ninth century (Afsaruddin, 2020, p. 941). She studied biographical dictionaries on women from various periods, which, 'being more descriptive than prescriptive in its compositional intent, gives us more realistic accounts of the lives of the women depicted' (Afsaruddin, 2020, p. 942). Based on Shams al-Dīn Muhammad al-Sakhāwī's (832/1428 – 902/1497) *Kitāb al-Nisā'* (The Book of Women), Afsaruddin challenges the rather 'streamlined, monolithic, and perennially pessimistic image of medieval Muslim women' that emerges in certain kinds of contemporary literature (Afsaruddin, 2020, p. 942).

Kitāb al-Nisā' is the last volume of al-Sakhāwī's encyclopedic biographical work, *al-Daw' al-Lāmi' li-ahl al-Qarn al-Tāsi'* (The Brilliant Light Belonging to the People of the Ninth Century). It includes the biographies of the most notable 1,075 women of the Mamluk period (1250–1517) and, accordingly, offers comprehensive insights into the economic, social, and cultural aspects of women's existence during that period, including information about their educational pursuits and notable scholastic accomplishments (Al-Sahāwī, 1966, vol. 12).

These women referred to by al-Sahāwī are distinguished by their religious piety, as well as their dedication and excellence in religious education. Girls and women are frequently depicted as studying alongside boys, men, and other women. Upon obtaining their teaching credentials, a significant number of these Mamluk female scholars continued to instruct both men and women. Hence, Afsaruddin proposes that there was no gender restriction on the acquisition of knowledge during the Mamluk period (Al-Sahāwī, 1966, vol. 12; Afsaruddin, 2020, pp. 943–944). Al-Sahāwī himself, who lived in the fifteenth century, studied with about sixty-eight women, receiving *ijāzas* from about forty-six of them (Afsaruddin, 2020, p. 948). These historical realities well-documented by al-Sahāwī question the oversimplified notion of the gradual loss of women's rights for education and occupation the Qur'an originally granted her due to the heavy influence of customary rules of various local communities on Islamic practice.

Esposito suggests that, over time, as Islam expanded to various lands, the interaction and conflict between the Qur'anic reforms and the rigid social norms of the new converts led to new cultural changes that ultimately degraded women's status in Muslim societies (Esposito, 1975, p. 107). In this way, elements of Syrian, Mesopotamian, Persian, Egyptian, and Byzantine cultures infiltrated into Muslims' shared norms and principles. Rashda Sharif, who conducted several studies on gender issues in Islam, also attributes the restricted position of women in later Muslim history to Persian and Byzantine influences, particularly the practices of veiling and secluding women, both of which had Persian and possibly Byzantine roots (Sharif, 1987, p. 29; Keddie, 1990, p. 85). Due to seclusion, women ultimately stopped participating in the activities of the local mosques, which were also hubs of learning, intellectual growth, and civic engagement. Thus, over centuries, women gradually were forced to live lives of severe cultural deprivation and complete economic dependence on men. Since many fields, notably the natural sciences, require travelling to find experts and renowned scholars to learn profound knowledge from them, as well as lengthy periods of learning and training, all these factors rendered it hard for women to pursue education and careers in science. Hence, as noted by Esposito, 'The narrowing of the scope of their mobility and duties relegated all women to the role of simple domestic, uneducated and dependent psychologically, economically and socially on their menfolk' (Esposito, 1975, p. 108).

Nevertheless, it is impossible to make broad generalisations about the circumstances of Muslim women across the medieval and pre-modern Islamic world. *Kitāb al-Nisā'* provides descriptive and realistic accounts of the lives of the women of the fifteenth-century Mamluk society, demonstrating that seclusion, the prohibition of women from travelling, particularly without a male member of the family, and the deprivation of women's rights for education and attending mosques were not always the norm (Afsaruddin, 2020, p. 940). Some of these women depicted by al-Sahāwī' as the most notable and educated persons of his time travelled quite far and wide in their scholarly quest. For example, Fāṭima bt. Muḥammad b. 'Abd al-Hādī obtained teaching certificates (*ijāza*) in Damascus, Egypt, Aleppo, Hama, Homs, and other places of the Islamic world (al-Sahawi, 1966, vol. 12, p. 103; Afsaruddin, 2020, p. 946).

Almost without exception, the women depicted in *Kitāb al-Nisā'* were either born into families that were already distinguished for their tradition of learning or were from elite backgrounds. Furthermore, male family members are identified as motivating them to pursue their education (Afsaruddin, 2020, p. 945). Afsaruddin further recaps:

> Most male scholars of the period appeared to have little reservations, if any, about consorting with and benefitting from the erudition of a female scholar who had earned her degree and proved her scholarly mettle. They gratefully remembered the debt they owed these accomplished women and acknowledged their expertise in their written works. It is we who have consigned these remarkable women to relative oblivion and have, in effect, written them out of the master narrative of the production of knowledge in the Islamic milieu. Reinstating their roles in this crucial activity means reinstating a crucial block in the construction of the mighty edifice of medieval Islamic scholarship. (Afsaruddin, 2020, p. 957)

In summary, the practices of seclusion and the deprivation of women from the rights to education and travelling were not always the norm in every Muslim society. The original Qur'anic norms regarding gender roles, considered progressive at the time of Revelation, contributed to a societal framework that supported the flourishing of female education and potentially scientific pursuits.

4.2 Matters Related to Historical Documentation

As the historical analysis of Muslim women's participation in science and scholarship revealed in the previous part, there were far fewer women than males who can claim to be the leading actors in scientific transformations during the productive age of Islamic civilisation. Along with other possible causes, three of them will be covered in this section.

First, for a variety of cultural, political, and customary reasons, women had less access to education and employment than males. Based on available historical evidence and biographical dictionaries, we can assume that the number of highly educated and scientifically trained women was notably low in Islamic history, especially in regions that were distant from the ruling courts.

It is genuinely debatable whether Muslim societies, which posit women's inferior status, represent the Islamic ideal. In other words, is there any connection between Islam and the lack of access to education and mobility for women in Muslim societies? If the answer is affirmative, it begs the following question: Are the demands of the modern world and Islamic tradition inherently in conflict with one another?

These questions are pertinent given the widespread perception, fostered by practices like the veiling (*burqa*) and seclusion (*purdah*) of women, that 'Islam is a religion that grants no rights to women but rather prescribes their total subjugation to men' (Esposito, 1975, p. 100). John Esposito responds to this widely held opinion by saying that such a situation reflects neither the original spirit nor the content of the Qur'an which had enacted many reforms to improve women's debased position in pre-Islamic society (Esposito, 1975. p. 100).

Most of the social and legal practices perpetuating women's low standing such as the restriction of women's rights to travel or public involvement were actually influenced by the social customs and traditions that were common in the majority of ancient and medieval societies. Once these customs infiltrated Islamic culture and then became adopted as norms, they were inevitably associated with Islam. Then, once they were associated with Islam, they were seen as inflexible, if not sacred, social norms (Esposito, 1975, p. 100).

In this line, however, Amira Sonbol, a contemporary scholar in Islamic and Middle Eastern studies at Georgetown University, notes that, while making men and women equally responsible for their actions and salvation in the eyes of God, 'medieval *fiqh* elaborated an official Islamic ideal that considered women the weaker sex in need of protection' (Sonbol, 2003, p. 7). Interestingly, even though the Qur'an has no concept of original sin, in reality, sin was laid on the shoulders of women by the medieval *fiqh* discourse of the woman's entire body as '*awra* (the intimate parts of a human body that must be covered by clothing), and, consequently: 'When she goes out, she is accompanied by the devil' (al-Jabrī, 1975, pp. 92–93), and 'she must be secluded to protect man from her' (Sonbol, 2003, p. 8). Yet, Sonbol suggests that medieval discourse in *fiqh* books must be interpreted as the efforts of *fuqahā'* to establish a moral code, rather than as a representation of the actual life of women during that era: 'While *fiqh* literature gives the impression that women were secluded, the concrete evidence of women's lives from the medieval period onwards shows the continued role that women played in the productive and social life of their communities throughout the Islamic world' (Sonbol, 2003, p. 7). For instance, full veiling (*burqa*) has been both a class phenomenon and an urban one (Keddie & Baron, 1991, p. 3). This practice in the past was observed primarily among high-status and wealthy Muslim women, while lower-class ordinary Muslim women did not practice such seclusion (Mohammadi & Hazeri, 2020, p. 682). The practices of seclusion and *burqa* were not always the norm in every Muslim society, particularly among the commoners, and women continued to be active in the fields of religious studies and education.

The egalitarian aspect of Islam became a cultural norm during the earlier period of Islamic civilisation. For instance, the last (eighth) volume of *Kitāb al-Ṭabaqāt al-Kabīr* (The Major Book of Classes) by Muḥammad Ibn Sa'd (d. 230/845) from the ninth century is entirely devoted to well-known and productive women of the Prophet's time, his Companions, and a few of the Tabi'in, such as Umm Kulthum, the wife of Umar b. al-Khattab's grandson, covering a list of over 600 biographies of famous women of that era in total (Ibn Sa'd, vol. 8; Abou-Taleb, 2012, pp. 27–28). Various later biographical dictionaries such as *Tarīkh Madīnat Dimashq: Tarājim al-Nisā'* by Ali b. al-Ḥasan ibn Asākīr (d. 571/1176), *Ṣifāt al-Ṣafwah* by 'Abd al-Rahmān al-Jawzī (d. 597/1201), *Tadhkirat al-Awliya* by Farīd al-Dīn 'Aṭṭār (d. 628/1230), and *al-Iṣāba fī Tamyīz al-Ṣaḥāba* by al-'Asqalānī (d. 852/1449) also provide a substantial amount of information about women, mostly the female companions of the Prophet. As we already highlighted, women, especially the elites, did not have serious restrictions on knowledge-seeking and occupation. Ibn Jarir al-Tabari (839–923), a prolific polymath during the first centuries of the Abbasid rule, for example, ruled that a woman might qualify for the post of a judge (*qadi*) without any restriction (Waddy, 1980, p. 4), confirming the actual realisation of women's professional opportunities if they were qualified.

In Muslim Spain, Umayyad society also provided women fairness and opportunities. The elevated status that women held under Arab rule in Spain, as exemplified by Scott, 'gave them an influence, and invested them with an importance, elsewhere unknown in the Mohammedan world' of that time (Scott, 1904, vol. 3, p. 446). Muslim chronicles on Andalusia such as *al-Dhakīra fī Maḥāsin Ahl al-Jazira* of Ibn Bassām (d. 542/1147), *Kitāb al-Ṣila* of Ibn Bashkuwāl (d. 579/1183), and *Al-Mughrib fī Ḥulā al-Maghrib* of Ibn Sa'īd (d. 684/1286) mention a considerable number of literate Andalusian women who were well-known for their poetry, wit, and knowledge (Kudsieh, 2003, p. 10). According to some historical accounts, Andalusian women had access to higher education, and career prospects, and played significant roles in their society's intellectual life. For instance, more than 170 literate women could be found in some of the city's suburbs during the reign of Al-Hakam II (r. 961–976), who were responsible for copying priceless manuscripts (Hershman et al., 2021, p. 126). Ibn Hazm (994–1064), a well-known Andalusian polymath who lived around the same time period, notes in the introduction to his *Tawq al–Hamāmah* (The Ring of the Dove) that most of his teachers were women: 'I never sat with men until I was already a youth and my beard had begun to sprout' (Waddy, 1980, p. 78). These few cases demonstrate that not merely royal women but also ordinary women were highly educated and actively involved in Andalusian intellectual and scholarly life.

Instances of outstanding women continued to appear in many parts of the Muslim rule, particularly within the royal family. For example, during the Mamluk dynasty, women continued to be distinguished for their religious piety, excellence, and dedication to knowledge as al-Sahāwī's work depicts more than a thousand notable women who were actively involved in educational and scholarly activities (Afsaruddin, 2020, p. 944). Even in Ottoman society, which is presumed to have practiced gender segregation at its height, rural women continued to work in the fields alongside males (Waddy, 1980, p. 123), although they had few opportunities for education and the majority of women remained ignorant. Nevertheless, even throughout the period of total seclusion (from the sixteenth century until the Tanzimat era), some Ottoman women engaged in business, practised medicine, and worked in social welfare (Taskiran, 1976; Waddy, 1980, p. 124). Lady Mary Wortley Montagu, the wife of a British ambassador to Istanbul from 1716 to 1718, observed that Turkish elite women had greater freedom than women in Britain at the time during her visit to Istanbul in 1716 (Waddy, 1980, pp. 127–128).

Hence, we can infer that Muslim elite women and nobility had a greater opportunity to receive privileged education, expert training, and scholarly engagements as their families could afford to hire the best private teachers and specialists for their daughters and sisters. Furthermore, women continued to excel in and contribute to the fields where learning did not necessitate lengthy travel and residing in other regions through expertise and skill training. Thus, there are more instances of Muslim women who practised medicine compared to other branches of the natural sciences. Perhaps, the nature of studying medicine in medieval Islam paved the way for women in this regard. Pormann and Savage-Smith listed the four most important avenues for studying medicine in the Muslim world as being familial tuition, apprenticeship, attendance at *majlises* (public sessions at local mosques), and hospital training, while *madrasahs* constituted venues for medical education only occasionally (Pormann & Savage-Smith, 2007, p. 83). There was no need to travel long distances to study medicine under a specific scholar as every suburb of large cities or even comparatively small towns had a *bimaristan* alongside local medical schools. Therefore, entering the medical area was far more safe, feasible, and comfortable for women than entering the fields of engineering or astronomy. Nevertheless, some women travelled quite far and wide in their scholarly quest as al-Sahāwī's biographical records demonstrate (al-Sahāwī, 1966, vol. 12, p. 947).

Another important observation is that Muslim women who were noted in historical records as accomplished scientists and scholars were from elite backgrounds or well-educated families (Afsaruddin, 2020, p. 945) and were frequently mentioned along with the names of their well-known brothers, fathers, or sons. In other words, most successful women's names were noted secondarily because they came from nobility or because they had successful fathers, husbands, sons, or brothers. Therefore, the number of Muslim female scientists and intellectuals may have been far higher, but they were mostly ignored in historical accounts due to their non-elite status. This argument indicates a serious problem with gender bias in historical narrations as highlighted by Rashda Sharif that 'male interpretations of Islam have suited male interests' (Sharif, 1987, p. 29).

It seems that those who recorded historical happenings were unconcerned about women, except the most influential ones attributable to their family's nobility and social ranking. The whole picture of the role of Muslim women in history is thus quite challenging to establish. Nevertheless, al-Sahāwī's biographical dictionary could be an exception as most of the women mentioned in his work completed their education before their marriage. While a handful of women did remain unmarried, in most cases, women continued their academic life after marriage and taught both sexes (Afsaruddin, 2020, p. 954).

However, historians did show great enthusiasm to record a large number of women in the early period of Islam, their achievements, lifestyles, and attitudes, particularly of those who lived during the time of the Prophet and the following few generations as moral exemplars for the following Muslim societies. Over the centuries, as women started to experience unequal treatment due to the penetration of local customs into religious norms and resulting changes, society tended to isolate them and refrain from discussing their accomplishments, perhaps, out of fear of moral indecency and a lack of chastity (Abou-Bakr et al., 2021). Additionally, writers were primarily interested in documenting the histories of royalty and well-known people although there were exceptions. Hence, there may have been more female scientists, scholars, and medical professionals who are not included in the history books because they did not come from the elite or were dealing with the education or healthcare of ordinary people.

Peter E. Pormann questioned the validity of medical treatises written about female patients and practitioners in the medieval Muslim world since 'they (women) constituted roughly half the population, we may rightly ask how they experienced disease and accessed health care. In the theoretical literature, women appear mostly in two contexts, that of disorders specific to women; and that of disease that affect women differently from men' (Pormann, 2009, p. 1599). After providing a brief historical journey through medieval Islamic medicine, he concluded that

> [women] often found themselves marginalised within medieval Muslim societies, and their voice only reaches us faintly through the opacity of male bias. And yet, their story can also teach us a lesson today. In both the medical and the non-medical modern literature, one often finds statements in which male authorities, be they medical or religious, make absolute claims about what is, or is not, permissible in Islam. Not infrequently such statements serve the purpose of curtailing women's freedom. Yet if we look at Islam both diachronically and synchronically – that is to say, in all its historical depth and present breadth, in its former variations and current manifestations – we see a picture of great diversity. (Pormann, 2009, p. 1599)

Hence, an existing postulation about Muslim women's contributions to science and scholarship reflects a set of partial and insufficient thoughts that resulted from the dearth of historical data and supporting evidence related to Muslim history. There is always a great possibility that historical occurrences or activities may not have been accurately or fully represented, or its larger picture and details were not deemed by medieval chroniclers deserving of recording in the official chronicles. Thus, Tarif Khalidi, a professor of Arabic at the American University of Beirut, suggests viewing medieval historical works and biographical dictionaries as products of the thought of the reporters' era rather than being a primary source of the earlier Islamic past (Khalidi, 1973, p. 53). Islamic historical narratives on influential women such as *al-Tabaqāt* of Ibn Sa'd were recorded centuries after the actual events. Hence biographical dictionaries reflected the author's 'own biases with regards to sorting, filtering, organising, and narrating the data at hand' (Abou-Taleb, 2012, p. 1). The status of women in early Islamic history, consequently, was depicted exclusively through a pen of men who lived centuries after the actual events in a setting, where the perfect model of a desired Muslim woman became already moulded based on the tribal and social customs (Abou-Taleb, 2012, pp. 5–8).

Having said that, we must also acknowledge that just a tiny portion of the accessible Islamic manuscripts have been studied up to the present day. Referring to Islamic jurisprudence, Professor of Law at the University of California El Fadl noted:

It is fair to say that considering the wealth of historical and legal sources that are yet to be studied, edited, or published, our understanding of gender dynamics and of the way that these dynamics influenced the development of Islamic jurisprudence is still in its nascent stages. One of the most startling facts, for instance, is that despite reports that some women jurists wrote as much as a 60-volume treatise on Islamic law (Kahhala, 1959, vol. 2, p. 45) very few, if any, of those manuscripts authored by female legal scholars have been published. It is somewhat ironic that Islamic jurisprudence, including the issue of gender and its interplay with law, has been a victim of its own importance. (Abou El Fadl, 2003, p. 41)

4.3 Gender Disparity in Light of Historical Context

Discussions in the previous pages emphasised how women in medieval and pre-modern Islamic history had fewer access to possibilities for education, employment, and participation in scholarly pursuits than males did. Having said that, before drawing hasty conclusions and attributing such discrimination to the nature of Islam, it is essential to reconsider the existing lifestyles, customs, and realities of that time. The inferior status of women in pre-modern societies was not unique in the Muslim world alone. Not much is known about the contributions made by women not only in Islam but also in European history and other parts of the world (Gelbart, 2016, pp. 116–127).

A natural philosopher of the twentieth century, Sir Alan Cook, suggests that women started engaging in natural philosophy and science in Europe during the age of the scientific revolution around the mid-seventeenth to mid-eighteenth centuries. He writes, 'Eight ladies certainly had some part in the scientific revolution, not just as tricoteuses watching the heads roll, but themselves helping to bring down the guillotine upon Aristotelians, Cartesians, astrologers, hermetics and mystics' (Sir Alan Cook, 1997: 2). Cook mentions the names of Katherine Lady Ranelagh (1615–1691), Queen Christina of Sweden (1629–1689), Elizabeth Hevelius, Lady Masham (1658–1708), Catherine Barton (1679–1739), Queen Caroline (1683–1737), Emilie Du Chatelet (1706–1749), and Nicole-Reine Lepaute (1723–1788) as the first examples of European women in science, even though these ladies' contributions had too little impact on the rapidly advancing scientific development. Instead, most of them assisted their husbands, fathers, or other male relatives who were eminent scientists at the time and influenced scientific development in different ways. As Cook concludes, 'Each of them also, in different ways, seems to have made life for their friends and colleagues more agreeable, more interesting, more elegant and more refined' (Cook, 1997, p. 11). All these ladies belonged to royal or elite societies and were widowed at young ages.

Hence, an inadequate engagement of women in science and scholarship in pre-modern societies was not an issue that primarily affected Muslims alone. The reasons for unjust treatment of women differed in various cultures and societies. In the Muslim world, it was primarily influenced by the customs of the time which prioritised the safety and chastity of women. In a traditional Muslim family unit, the husband and other male relatives were the undisputed breadwinners, and the education of daughters was thus seen as pointless because they were never expected to work outside the household. In many traditional Muslim communities today, there still remains a negative attitude against women's access to education and employment. This negative attitude is articulated or even justified by some radical interpretations of Islamic texts. In many extreme communities, such as Boko Haram in Nigeria and the Taliban in Afghanistan and Pakistan, it transcends mere 'attitude' and has become codified as legislation.

Women's participation in medieval Europe's sciences was restricted due to men barring women from science systematically and appropriating sciences as being 'masculine' (Allred, 2016, p. 14). Women were viewed as agents for reproduction alone, whereas production and science-related activities were regarded beyond their physical and mental biological abilities. This view has echoed in Europe for centuries through language, rhetoric, and philosophy. Meanwhile, only men were seen as capable of the creation of thought and ideas (Allred, 2016, pp. 2–3).

The misconception of the biological inferiority of women has its roots in Greek philosophy. Aristotle (384 BC–322 BC), the great Greek philosopher and polymath with contributions to nearly every field of human knowledge, equated activity with masculinity and inactivity with femininity. The 'coldness … would not permit [their] menstrual blood to perfect itself as semen', according to Aristotle, making women stunted males (Merchant, 1980, p. 13; Allred, 2016, p. 15). This implies that women were assumed to be inferior to males biologically even though the Greeks had several goddesses and priestesses who embodied different aspects of life and nature, such as Athena, the goddess of wisdom, and Aphrodite, the goddess of love and beauty. Being a woman in Greek society still meant being at a huge disadvantage, although the position of women varied significantly amongst city states. Women in Athens, protected by Athena (ironically, a goddess of feminine derivation), were primarily expected to focus on household duties, were subject to their fathers or husbands' authority, and were unable to possess property or vote. Hence, democracy was limited to wealthy male citizens, while women were not considered citizens. Sparta, on the other hand, provided women with greater freedom and responsibilities (Seitkasimova, 2019, pp. 53–54). Spartan women were allowed to own property, obtain an education, and were required to maintain physical fitness to bear healthy offspring. Hence, although there were exceptions, Greek culture predominantly relegated women to an inferior status relative to men, with their principal responsibilities centred on domestic and familial duties.

Some treatises from the Enlightenment age still shared the same attitude towards women in Europe. Assuming that women are not equal to men, Pierre Roussel (1742–1802), a French journalist, argued in his *Système Physique et Moral de la Femme* that women were biologically frail because this attribute sustained the population, with males serving as the inventors and women serving as caretakers (Vila, 1995, p. 78). According to Allred, any woman who questioned this caretaker position was viewed as disorderly, a witch in the public eye (Allred, 2016, p. 12).

Such dogmas and traditions rendered it nearly impossible for women to participate in scientific activities and thought production in the medieval and early modern periods of European history. Hence, another way that Christian and Islamic philosophy differ is that, even though women were also given caregiving responsibilities in Islam, Muslim scholars never questioned the cognitive abilities of women. Islam holds both men and women to be equally capable in scholarship and science, despite the fact that, throughout Islamic history, women were frequently denied access to advanced levels of education due to traditions, circumstances, and familial obligations (Abdelgafar, 2024, p. 66). Interestingly, Muslim and Jewish women offered their services in the Western European medical market as surgeons, optometrists, barbers, herbalists, or simply as 'healers' (*metgessa, medica, miresse,* or *arztzatin*) between the twelfth and fifteenth centuries. As Monica H. Green, an expert on gender history at Arizona State University claims, 'Muslims and Jews were seen to provide more specialised obstetrical care than was on offer in Christian communities' (Green, 2008b, p. 111).

Few women were already allowed into scholarship during the lifetime of Isaac Newton (1642–1726) as patrons or observers, letting them develop their knowledge. They were still not regarded as being on par with men as inventors, but their participation was tolerated merely for their personal progression. For instance, the English poet Mary Chudleigh (1656–1710) thought that knowledge would raise her from her femininity and finally transform her into a complete being. In 1678, Lena Lucrezia Cornaro Piscopia became the world's first female graduate, earning a degree in philosophy from the University of Padua. Nevertheless, women's participation was still minimal (Allred, 2016, pp. 13–14).

Between the twelfth and the fifteenth centuries, universities started to appear throughout Europe. Women were mostly forbidden from attending universities and men were taught that women should be restricted from science and education. This was especially the case in the field of medicine, as its philosophy and logic were formulated with an emphasis on the writings of Galen and Hippocrates, two ancient Greek philosophers who held that women were physically and mentally inferior to men. Colleges and professional schools for women started to appear in the USA and Europe in the eighteenth century, paving the route to employment and financial independence for women although female higher education was not publicly encouraged until the early twentieth century. Particularly in the UK, women were not allowed to enrol in public universities until 1920 (Tienxhi, 2017, p. 1). While speaking about female scientists in America before 1920, Rossiter highlighted the lack of awareness in contemporary American society for two reasons. First, 'women scientists are still isolated phenomena' and, second, 'it is only very recently that women in America have begun to take up careers in science' (Rossiter, 1974, p. 312). Women soon appeared in the scientific community as professors and scientists, albeit they were still expected to not do as well as their male counterparts (Allred, 2016, p. 18). Since then, various conducts have been made to combat prejudice against women both in the workplace and in society at large.

Hence, the central determination of feminist movements that evolved in the West was directed towards confronting stereotypes about women's inferior nature, both mentally and biologically, as well as widespread discrimination against women in the workplace and at institutions of higher learning. The causes for gender disparity in the Muslim world are not necessarily the same as in the West. Thus, we should refrain from envisaging Muslim communities to be exactly the same as medieval and early modern European societies, thereby grounding the potential solutions to prejudices against women against a Western model. Perhaps today's misconceptions, such as connecting gender disparity in some modern Muslim societies to Islam (Mcclendon et al., 2018, pp. 3–4) or presuming that religious Muslim women are forbidden from careers in the sciences, are the result of this Eurocentric approach that models Christianity for Islam, and medieval religious society in Europe for Muslim societies.

4.4 Gender-Related Educational Limitations in the Modern Muslim World

This and the next discussion of the Element concentrate on the issues that are related to contemporary Muslim women's engagements in science. While speaking about modern Muslims' engagement in the scientific project in general, Hillel Ofek stated that today 'the spirit of science in the Muslim world is as dry as the desert'. He further continued that 'forty-six Muslim countries combined contribute just 1 percent of the world's scientific literature' (Ofek, 2011).

However, our primary goal here is not to explore every aspect of the scientific underdevelopment of the contemporary Muslim world. Instead, the discussion is constructed around two issues. The first one highlights the reasons that contribute to the underdeveloped training of female scientists in the Muslim world and contends that the chances and potential for female representation in academia are already severely compromised at the fundamental stages of education in underdeveloped nations. The challenges surrounding the underrepresentation of female scientists, particularly in STEM-related academia and research, are addressed in the following section.

The lack of scientific production in the Muslim world is primarily related to the lack of proper professional training and educational competency of youth. It takes years of effective training, the development of resources, and a supportive educational environment to develop productive scientists. Thus, in order to investigate the causes of the original knowledge production-related limitations in the Muslim world, particularly the inadequate engagement of Muslim women in science, we must comprehend the national schooling attainment of each country, its educational tradition, and the public attitude towards girl's education and scientific engagements.

There are various distinctive, complicated attitudes on girls' education and their employment in STEM-related fields in the contemporary Muslim world. These attitudes are a result of significant political, intellectual, religious, social, and historical conditions and formations (Hassan, 2000, p. 55). In comparison to women in other nations, women in the Middle East and other Muslim-majority countries 'tend to have fewer years of schooling on average, lower rates of labour force participation, less representation in politics, and wider gender gaps on these measures', according to research by David Mcclendon, a former research associate who focused on religion research at Pew Research Center, and his colleagues (Mcclendon et al., 2018, p. 2). Many factors account for the gender gap in the workplace and education.

For instance, public schools, teachers, and especially girls' education became a target of violence and crimes by extremist groups and military gangs like Boko Haram in Nigeria and the Taliban in Afghanistan and Pakistan, who claim that Western-type school education is forbidden in Islam and that gender equality infringes on traditional Islamic values. Such realities, which disproportionately affect girls and prevent them from receiving even a basic education, are likely to damage their potential possibilities and prospects for years to come. It is also pointless to discuss the potential of women's participation in STEM areas in these war-affected nations because any success in these fields demands many years of consistent educational training, as well as science- and gender-friendly provisions both at the workplace and in public.

Moreover, blatant gender discrimination against women in some Muslim societies raises concerns about the religion's role in promoting gender disparity and Islam's impact on women's access to higher education. Some Muslim societies tend to have more conservative views on sexuality and gender, which may restrain women's educational ambitions and prospects, both in the past and the present (Fish, 2002, pp. 24–25; Mcclendon et al., 2018, p. 4). Even in nations where females are encouraged to attend school, some prevalent practices like early marriage and childbearing interfere with girls' education (Youssef, 1976–1977, p. 199). Thus, while flaws in girls' education are primarily related to the absence of proper infrastructure, the availability of educational options does not ensure their utilisation (Bowman & Anderson, 1980, p. S14).

Mcclendon's research on educational attainment by religion for women and men in 151 countries found that 'Islam is not restricting Muslim women's educational attainment, at least not globally' (Mcclendon et al., 2018, p. 24). Gender norms, particularly those pertaining to family laws like marriage, divorce, and custody, are founded on irrelevant and out-of-date interpretations of Islam that had been instituted many centuries back. The negative impact of various centuries-old local pre-Islamic customs on the interpretation of Islam that had been perceived relevant to that particular time and context has already been highlighted in earlier pages. Contemporary societies that still consider these historical interpretations of Islam as applicable to the present day uphold the centuries-old traditional gender norms while utterly disregarding the massive lifestyle and social changes that have taken place (Rahman, 2012) or even consider them a threat to a lifestyle that they believe is worth preserving as a means of protecting and implementing appropriate religious doctrine. The major concern here is that despite the Qur'an's silence on these particularities and its overall opposition to gender inequality and discrimination, these traditions and customs are frequently perceived as being fundamental to Islam. Hence, as Barazangi observes, primarily because of patriarchal readings of the Qur'an and the entire range of early Qur'anic literature, Muslim women have remained a passive force in constructing contemporary Islamic thought as well as scholarship (Barazangi, 2008–2009, p. 5).

Muslim women's participation in education is influenced by conservative sexual and gender standards in a variety of ways. First, girls' education could be interrupted by early marriage and childbirth, which lowers their level of educational attainment. In addition, because girls are expected to marry young, their families 'may see little need to invest in their daughters' education, especially if the financial and opportunity costs are high and gender segregation of the labour market offers little hope for strong economic returns' (Lehrer, 1999; Mcclendon et al., 2018, p. 5). Finally, the state's policies and its distribution of resources for women's education and research may be influenced by the general public attitude about gender. In the long run, these obstacles will make it extremely difficult for women to become scientists or to undertake scientific research in conservative societies.

Not only outdated customs and detrimental historical legacies but different recent political and economic factors also contribute to gender disparities. Girls have poorer access to education, even at the most basic levels, in war-torn countries like Yemen, Afghanistan, Iraq, Somalia, Sudan, and Syria. According to our case study of five states, Muslim women have made considerable strides in reducing the gender gap, achieving female educational success, and contributing to scientific breakthroughs in countries with greater political stability like Malaysia, Turkey, Qatar, and Jordan, while female educational settings and chances are depressing in the economically and politically unstable Pakistan. Hence, political and economic stability is crucial for Muslim women's access to higher education and science-based training.

Hence, we may specify a correlation between the levels of women's educational engagement and the country's structural and economic limitations. The Muslim-majority countries are located in Africa, Southern Asia, Central Asia, and the Middle East, which are less developed economically and democratically than other regions. Access to education, school resources, and educational quality are all important factors in determining how far girls advance in schooling and are all affected by economic development and country income.

According to Mcclendon, young Muslim women living in wealthier countries have more years of education and are more likely to hold advanced degrees. He claims that gender discrimination in family laws, democracy, and religious affiliation does not greatly affect the educational performance of young Muslim women in economically more advanced countries like Qatar, Malaysia, Kuwait, Saudi Arabia, Algeria, and Tunisia (Mcclendon et al., 2018, pp. 19–20). As a result, women experience remarkable educational advancements in nations that are rapidly developing economically, and gender equality in these nations is also improving greatly. For instance, young girls in Saudi Arabia attend school for an average of 11.5 years, which puts them on par with Muslim women who reside in Western nations. Hence, productive and long-lasting engagement of women in education, scholarship, and occupation cannot be attained in the absence of good governance, economic development, and political stability.

4.5 Contemporary Muslim Women in STEM

Young Muslim women in economically developed nations such as Qatar, Jordan, Malaysia, and Turkey are more likely to have more years of education and advanced degrees, including in STEM professions. Since the 1990s, global enrolment trends have produced a reverse gender gap, with more women than males enrolling in higher education. For instance, in Malaysia, the ratio of male to female students in public universities was 1:1.6 in 2018 (38.08% male to 61.92% female) (Ministry of Education Malaysia, 2018, p. 35). The number of female students at Qatar University has been roughly twice the number of male students since 2012.[30]

A reverse gender gap has also been detected in a number of Muslim countries when it comes to STEM fields. For instance, women earn more than half of all degrees in science and math in the Middle East and several other Muslim nations, including Iran, Malaysia, and Uzbekistan.[31] Research conducted by Omar Bataineh, associate professor in Education Foundations at the Hashemite University of Jordan, and his colleagues, found that several 'Arab nations, including Egypt, Jordan, and the UAE, have given a high priority to STEM education not only to improve performance in international comparative studies but also to encourage enrolment and participation in STEM-related fields' (Bataineh et. al., 2022, p. 2). Notably, according to UNESCO, women make up to 57 per cent of STEM graduates in Arab nations.[32]

Women in many Muslim countries earn more degrees in science and math per capita than their counterparts in the USA and Europe, as *Study International* suggests.[33] For instance, only 35 per cent of undergraduate STEM degrees in the USA are earned by women, while only 18.4 per cent of bachelor's degrees in engineering are awarded to women, and they make up between 8 and 34 per cent of the engineering workforce.[34] To compare, the rates of Jordanian female students for engineering and computer science are respectively around 28 per cent and 45 per cent as of 2021. In addition, more than 60 per cent of Jordanian students majoring in the natural sciences, medicine, dentistry, and pharmacy are female.[35] Omar Bataineh and his colleagues' research also revealed that, as of 2022, the majority of students enrolled in engineering and

---

[30] Qazi, S. (2015). *In Qatar, Education Drives Workforce Shifts for Women*, www.al-fanarmedia.org/2015/08/in-qatar-education-drives-workforce-shifts-for-women/.

[31] Weingarten, E. (2017). *The STEM Paradox: Why Are Muslim-Majority Countries Producing So Many Female Engineers*, https://slate.com/human-interest/2017/11/the-stem-paradox-why-are-muslim-majority-countries-producing-so-many-female-engineers.html.

[32] Euronews. (2023). *STEM Pioneers: the UAE Women Empowering the Middle East*, www.euronews.com/next/2022/02/21/stem-pioneers-the-uae-women-empowering-the-middle-east.

[33] Study International. (2019). *The Rise of Women in STEM in the Arab World*, www.studyinternational.com/news/the-rise-of-women-in-stem-in-the-arab-world/.

[34] Euronews. (2023). *STEM Pioneers: the UAE Women Empowering the Middle East*, www.euronews.com/next/2022/02/21/stem-pioneers-the-uae-women-empowering-the-middle-east.

[35] UNESCO. (2022). *Jordanian Women Shine in Science*, www.unesco.org/en/articles/jordanian-women-shine-science.

computer sciences are male in Jordan, with a lesser extent in other fields. Female students represent the majority in the fields of health sciences and basic sciences. About 29 per cent of students who graduated with a degree in medical sciences are female, followed by engineering (28%), basic science (27%), and mathematics and computer science (16%) (Bataineh et al., 2022, p. 7).

Thus, the gender gap in STEM education that is present globally does not necessarily apply to economically developed Muslim nations. Muslim societies usually do not perceive STEM professions as being masculine but, rather, a vocation with a good wage for women if they need to work in the future. The main dilemma, nonetheless, is a widespread tendency for Muslim women's engagement in STEM fields to decrease sharply as education levels rise.[36] In the instance of Malaysia, Table 3 shows that the percentage of Muslim women declines as education levels rise (see Table 3).

Besides, the high number of STEM-related female graduates in the Muslim world does not necessarily translate into employment realities (Hassan, 2000, p. 56; Naguib, 2024, p. 14). In other words, even while Muslim women are motivated to pursue degrees in STEM subjects, these highly educated and qualified women are underrepresented in science-related industries. One of the key factors for this underrepresentation of women in the scientific sector is related to predominant social norms that emphasise marriage and childbearing for women. Since women are traditionally not encouraged to work outside their homes unless it is necessary to meet the family's financial needs, the potential productivity of a part of female human resources is missing in many Muslim societies.

In addition, traditionally male-dominated workplaces would rather prefer hiring a man than a woman even if she could be more competent for the job. In nations that are members of the Organisation for Economic Cooperation and Development (OECD), 71 per cent of STEM-related male graduates hold professional positions in the STEM sectors, compared to only 43 per cent of STEM-related female graduates.[37]

Despite the high percentage of women who pursue degrees, their participation in higher levels of scholarship, especially in research, dramatically declines. Consequently, research institutes and academia are mostly dominated by men throughout the Muslim world, especially at decision-making levels.

---

[36] UNESCO. (2015). *A Complex Formula: Girls and Women in Science, Technology, Engineering and Mathematics in Asia*, http://unesdoc.unesco.org/images/0024/002457/245717E.pdf.

[37] Scientific American. (2023). *Raising Gender Equality in STEM Careers*, www.scientificamerican.com/custom-media/a-new-dawn-for-innovation-in-qatar/raising-gender-equality-in-stem-careers.

Such circumstances may eventually result in less female-friendly policies, lower prospects for female applicants to receive scholarships and grants, as well as the passive position of women in the research environment.

The final point I wanted to make is that, despite cultural and regional differences in female involvement in STEM education, attracting more women into science-related research and occupations continues to be a common challenge across the entire world. Thus, the underrepresentation of educated women in academia, professional settings, and scientific research is not a problem that only affects Muslim nations (Villar & Guppy, 2015, p. 3). In 1961, Charles Percy Snow stated that Western society does not in reality 'regard women as suitable for scientific careers' (Snow, 1961, p. 57). Science is still considered a 'masculine world and the so-called "ivory tower" remains a male dominated place' (Tintori, 2017, p. 4). The underrepresentation of women in scientific careers remains a challenge. For instance, women make up over half of the workforce in America and earn more than half of the university degrees in biology, chemistry, and mathematics there. But according to the American Community Survey conducted by the US Census Bureau in 2019, only 30 per cent of STEM jobs were held by women as shown in Figure 3.[38]

To sum up, unfavourable public attitudes towards female scientists are a common challenge the world over. At the same time, we should applaud recent developments in many Muslim-majority nations, where women have achieved significant educational advances in the way of reducing the gender gap.

5 Conclusion

The picture that appears from an evaluation of Muslim women's contributions to the sciences in the past and present is a multifaceted one. In the classical era, the adoption of Qur'anic reforms significantly enhanced women's status in the family and society. The historical empowerment of women, however, bears little resemblance to the situation of women in modern Muslim communities, particularly in terms of educational attainment and professional competence in the STEM sectors. Our discussions on contributions made by Muslim women to scientific and technological developments in the past and today indicate the following concluding remarks.

First, even if we agree that Muslim women are less skilled and interested in STEM sectors compared to other contemporary women, we shall admit that it is not due to Islam. A recent study of women's empowerment by Rabia Naguib, an

---

[38] United States Census Bureau. (2019). *STEM and STEM-related Occupations by Sex and Median Earnings: ACS*, www.census.gov/data/tables/time-series/demo/income-poverty/stem-occ-sex-med-earnings.html.

Figure 3 Representation of Women in STEM Research Globally
Source: De Vasconcellos et al. (2022, p. 1)

associate professor at the Doha Institute for Graduate Studies in Qatar, suggests that 'Islam acts as a catalyst for women's empowerment' in contemporary Muslim societies (Naguib, 2024, p. 36). There are no religious restrictions rooted in the Qur'an that forbid women from pursuing a profession in science, whether as learners or experts. Nonetheless, some historical realities, public concerns about the safety of girls, as well as the infiltration of various types of non-Islamic cultures into the Muslim tradition caused significantly fewer women than men who can be recognised as the architects of the scientific production age in the Muslim past. To put it simply, subsequent historical events as well as assimilated cultural influences at times seriously compromised women's rights, making it almost impossible for them to pursue knowledge or work as scientists alongside men (Esposito, 1975, p. 113).

Besides, Islam places a strong emphasis on education for all individuals, regardless of gender. It emphasises reasoning, knowledge, and observations, which are the key components that are required for intellectual and scientific advancements. Various Qur'anic passages repeatedly instruct readers to seek knowledge, reflect, and contemplate natural occurrences to better appreciate God's might and wisdom. Thus, there could not be such kind of dichotomy between faith and science in Muslim scholarship and public attitude, which we usually observe in the case of medieval Europe. Rather, faith, intellectual, and scientific engagements were envisaged by Muslim scientists in a cohesive manner, ensuring the appearance of giants and polymaths in Islamic civilisation who shined as experts across multiple disciplines. Hence, the presumptions that have been mentioned earlier in the Introduction that scientific and technological activities are not permissible in Islam, or that Islam forbids women from participating in public life, including educational and scientific pursuits, appear to be doubtful.

Furthermore, the medieval European approach to women's education was shaped by the distinctive interplay between ecclesiastical authority and scientific inquiry, alongside prevailing notions of women's biological inferiority. Science was appropriated as being exceptionally 'masculine' (Allred, 2016, p. 14) up to the modern age, while women were viewed as agents for reproduction alone, incapable of the construction of ideas and scientific activities, both mentally and physically. Muslim scholars never questioned the cognitive abilities of women as Islam holds both men and women to be equally capable in scholarship and science. Besides, the inadequate engagement of modern Muslim women in science and the gender gap in STEM sectors are mostly caused by conservative norms on sexuality and gender, which are founded on traditional interpretations of Islam and local customs, as well as economic and political circumstances. Thus, it is impossible to imagine devout Muslim communities as being exactly like medieval and early modern European societies, and, therefore, it is inappropriate to construct any potential solutions to discrimination against women in the Muslim world on an exact model previously practiced in the West.

Third, it is also not practical to generalise the position of women in the Muslim world based on a few instances of injustices and abuses committed by the Taliban and Boko Haram regimes. There are numerous exceptional female Muslim scientists who are renowned both nationally and globally for their accomplishments and inventions, as can easily be found by simple online searches.

The Muslim world, both historically and at present, refers to a vast area with ethnically and culturally diversified communities although they all adhere to Islam. Each Muslim nation state is distinct, with its own ethnic and cultural diversity, traditions, historical realities, social and economic provisions, national priorities, and long-standing concerns (Charrad, 2011, p. 420). Therefore, we should refrain from drawing generalised conclusions about the entire Muslim world based on the existence of some countries with high gender gaps in educational attainment and job security while disregarding other examples of Muslim countries that have been successful in closing the gender gap.

Likewise, factors such as political stability, economic growth, and national income all affect girls' access to education, school resources, educational quality, and employment prospects. Girls have poorer access to education, even at the most basic levels, in war-torn nations like Yemen, Afghanistan,

Iraq, Somalia, Sudan, and Syria. In countries with greater political stability, such as Malaysia, Turkey, Qatar, and Jordan, Muslim women have made significant advancements in closing the gender gap, achieving female educational success, and contributing to scientific breakthroughs, while female educational opportunities and settings are depressing in the economically and politically unstable Pakistan. Hence, not the level of religiosity but the country's political and economic stability is crucial for Muslim women's access to higher education and science-based training.

Fourth, in recent years, women have experienced remarkable educational advancements in Muslim nations that are developing economically, and gender equality in these nations' STEM sectors is also improving significantly. In many Muslim nations, enrolment trends have produced a reverse gender gap, with more women than men enrolling in higher education. In Malaysia, for example, women have exceeded men in the STEM areas at the BA and MA degree levels, with the exception of engineering. Turkey recently has also seen a 40 per cent increase in the proportion of female students majoring in STEM subjects.[39]

Having said that, the main dilemma begins at the higher stages of education, particularly the doctoral level. As education levels rise, Muslim women's participation in STEM professions falls substantially.[40] Furthermore, the large number of STEM-related female graduates in the Muslim world does not necessarily translate into employment realities. In other words, even while Muslim women are chasing degrees in STEM subjects, these highly educated qualified women are underrepresented in science-related industry and academia. This disparity appears to be shaped by the traditional social image of the job market preferences that favour hiring males for specific positions (Bataineh, 2022, p. 11).

Last, the study emphasises the necessity for immediate improvements in the entire Muslim world to revitalise general research culture through comprehensive social and educational reforms. Despite the recent improvements in Muslim women's educational attainment, it is still too early to anticipate the appearance of globally renowned research centres in the Muslim world with outstanding female scientists and inspired inventors in the upcoming years. We must accept that, in comparison to Western nations, the Muslim world has far fewer highly qualified scientists, both male and female. With a few notable exceptions, Muslim researchers do not lead in scientific breakthroughs with a global impact and broad implications. The most significant factors for

---

[39] Hürriyet. (2021). *Turkish Women Scientists' Ratio Surpasses EU Average, Data Shows*, www.hurriyetdailynews.com/turkish-women-scientists-ratio-surpasses-eu-average-data-shows-162600.

[40] UNESCO. (2015). *A Complex Formula: Girls and Women in Science, Technology, Engineering and Mathematics in Asia*, http://unesdoc.unesco.org/images/0024/002457/245717E.pdf.

low-quality research in contemporary Muslim countries include the persistence of outdated methods of teaching and learning like memorisation, the absence of academic and research training from the early stages of education and career development, and the lack of a scientific research culture in high schools and undergraduate university education. Outdated teaching techniques like memorisation or a failure to provide a space for kids to debate on real issues or carry out real-world investigations usually ruin the spirit of confidence and stimulus for new inquiries in young people. At the university level, students are not trained on how to think critically, taught how to express their ideas freely, and are not trusted with serious investigation responsibilities. All these factors significantly contribute to the inadequate research capacity and cognitive skills of potential researchers. Therefore, it is crucial to overhaul the educational system in general, and school curricula and teaching techniques in particular, in order to attain higher quality scientific achievements in the Muslim world, especially in countries, where girls are deprived of educational opportunities such as in Afghanistan, Pakistan, and Nigeria.

Hence, along with the attainment of gender parity in education and academia, Muslim states should concentrate on developing a young generation that is intellectually competent, capable of thinking critically and freely, and, most importantly, eager to bring positive changes to their societies. As such, the revival of scientific culture in contemporary Muslim societies necessitates a challenging but reachable path.

Furthermore, the consequences of new developments in the post-colonial Muslim world due to modernisation, as well as harnessing of science and technology with an increasing tendency towards industrialisation and urbanisation, have resulted in profound social changes, including changes in family structure, and, in particular, in woman's status and role in society. Thus, the Muslim public and states should recognise that gender norms and standards intended for medieval societies are no longer appropriate for contemporary social contexts. According to Esposito, unnecessary social gender inequalities in modern societies are caused by medieval attitudes and dominant social norms regarding women and the Muslim family (Esposito, 1975, pp. 100–101) that emphasise early marriages and childbearing, as well as seclusion for women.

As previously said, these obsolete societal gender and family norms are mostly rooted in local customs and theological traditions rather than presenting an Islamic ideal and the message of the Qur'an. Given that the Muslim family structure and realities have changed drastically in the twenty-first century, a germane interpretation of the Qur'an is essential to establish revised Islamic gender and family norms and rules that are both in line with the Qur'anic ideal and applicable to modern realities.

References

Abdelgafar, B. I. (2024). Re-envisioning Women's Empowerment: A Maqasid Approach to Understanding Women's Status and Rights in Islam. In Naguib, R., ed., *Women's Empowerment and Public Policy in the Arab Gulf States: Exploring Challenges and Opportunities*. Singapore: Springer, 55–73.

Abou-Bakr, O., As-Saa'dy, H. (2021). Female Physicians and Medical Profession in the Islamic History. *Khotwa For Documentation and Studies*, https://www.khotwacenter.com/female-physicians-and-medical-profession-in-the-islamic-history/.

Abou El Fadl, K. (2003). Legal and Jurisprudential Literature: 9th to 15th Century. In Joseph, S., ed., *Encyclopedia of Women and Islamic Cultures*, Vol. 1. Leiden: E. J. Brill, 37–41.

Abou-Taleb, A. (2012). *Gender Discourse in Kitab al-Tabaqat al-Kubra: Deconstructing Ibn Sa'd's Portrayal of the Model Muslim Woman*. Master's thesis, the American University in Cairo. AUC Knowledge Fountain. https://fount.aucegypt.edu/etds/872.

Abu Bakr, O. & Al-Sa'di, H. (1999). *Al-Nisa' Wa Mihnat Al-Tib Fi Al-Mojtama' at Al-Islamiyyah* [Women and Profession of Medicine in Muslim Societies]. Cairo: Multaqa al-Mar'ah wa al-Dhakirah.

Abou-Bakr, O. & As-Saa'dy, H. (2021). Female Physicians and Medical Profession in the Islamic History. *Khotwa For Documentation and Studies*, https://www.khotwacenter.com/female-physicians-and-medical-profession-in-the-islamic-history/.

Abu Rabi, I. (2005). Contemporary Islamic Intellectual History: A Theoretical Perspective. *Islamic Studies*, 44(4), 503–526.

Afsaruddin, A. (2003). Islamic Biographical Dictionaries: 11th to 15th Century. In Joseph, S., ed., Encyclopedia of Women and Islamic Cultures, Vol. 1. Leiden: E. J. Brill, 32–36.

Afsaruddin, A. (2020). Knowledge, Piety, and Religious Leadership in the Late Middle Ages: Reinstating Women in the Master Narrative. In Günther, S., ed., *Knowledge and Education in Classical Islam: Religious Learning Between Continuity and Change*, Vol. 2. Leiden: Brill, 941–962.

Afsaruddin, A. (2002). Reconstituting Women's Lives: Gender and the Poetics of Narrative in Medieval Biographical Collections. *The Muslim World*, 92(3 & 4), 461–480.

Ahmad, N., Ishak M. H., & Ali, M. F. (2020). Women's Rights in the Qur'an, Sunnah and Heritage of Islam. *Journal of Islam in Asia*, 17(3), 321–331. https://doi.org/10.31436/jia.v17i3.1004.

Ahmed, L. (1991). Early Islam and the Position of Women: The Problem of Interpretation. In Keddie, N. & Baron, B., eds., *Women in Middle Eastern History: Shifting Boundaries in Sex and Gender*. New Haven, CT: Yale University Press, 58–73.

Akhmetova, E. (2018). Abu Ali Ibn Sina. In Wain, A. & Kamali, M. H., eds., *Architects of Islamic Civilisation*. Kuala Lumpur: IAIS Malaysia, 108–15.

Akhmetova, E. (2016). Women in Islamic Civilisation: Their Rights and Responsibilities. *Islam and Civilisational Renewal*, 7(4), 476–491. https://doi.org/10.52282/icr.v7i4.230.

Akhmetova, E. (2015). Women's Rights: The Qur'anic Ideals and Contemporary Realities. *Islam and Civilisational Renewal*, 6(1), 58–75. https://doi.org/10.52282/icr.v6i1.356.

Al-Andalusi, A. (2015). The Rise and Decline of Scientific Productivity in the Muslim World: A Preliminary Analysis. *Islam and Civilisational Renewal*, 6(2), 229–246. https://doi.org/10.52282/icr.v6i2.333.

Al-ʿAsqalani, S. (1997). *Al-Durar al-Kamina fi Aʿyan al-Mia al-Thamina*, ed. ʿAbd al-Warith Muhammad Ali. Beirut: n.p.

Al-ʿAsqalani, S. (1968) *Al-Iṣābah fī Tamyīz al-Ṣahābah* (A Morning in the Company of the Companions). Cairo: Maktabat al-Kulliyyat al-Azhariyya.

Al-ʿAsqalani, Shihab al-Din Abi al-Fadl Ahmad ibn Ali Ibn Hajar. (1909). *Tahdhib al-Tahdhib*. Cairo: Dal al-Kitab al-Islami.

Al-Baghdadi, Al-Katib. (1931). *Tarikh Baghdad* [History of Baghdad], Vol. 6. Cairo: Happiness Press.

Al-Fanjari, A. S. (1980). *Rufaidah, Awwal Mumaridhat fi al-Islam* [Rufaidah, First Nurses in Islam]. Kuwait: Dar al Qalam.

Al-Ghazal, S. K. & Husain, M. (2021). Muslim Female Physicians and Healthcare Providers in Islamic History. *Journal of the British Islamic Medical Association*, 7(3), 1–8.

Al-Jabrī, ʿAbd al-Mutaʿāl Muhammad. (1975). *Al-Marʾa fī al-Tasawwur al-Islāmī*. Cairo: n.p.

Al-Jawzi, I. (1940). *Al-Muntazam fi ʾl-tarikh* [The Order in History], Vol.14. Haydarabad: Daʾirat al-Maʿarif al-Uthmaniya.

Allred, A. (2016). *Nature as Mother: Perceptions of Women in Science and the Natural World*. The USA: Guilford College.

Al-Mawardi, A. H. (1966). *Kitab al-Ahkam al-Sultaniyyah* [The Laws of Islamic Governance], 2nd ed. Cairo: Mustafa al-Babi al-Halabi.

Al-Sahāwī, M. b. ʿAbd al-Raḥmān. (1966). *Al-Dawʾ al-lāmiʿ li-ahl al-qarn al-tāsiʿ*. Beirut: n.p.

Al-Saʾeed, A. (1985). *Al-Tibb wa Raʾidatuhu Al-Muslimat* [Medicine and Its Pioneers among Muslim Women]. Amman: Dar al-Manar Linnashr.

References

As-Suyuti, J. (1994). *As-Suyuti's Medicine of the Prophet*. London: Ta-Ha Publishers Ltd.

Ayubi, Z. (2021). Authority and Epistemology in Islamic Medical Ethics of Women's Reproductive Health. *Journal of Religious Ethics*, 49(2), 245–269.

Bademci, G. (2006). First Illustrations of Female 'Neurosurgeons' in the Fifteenth Century by Serefeddin Sabuncuoglu. *Neurocirugía*, 17(2), 162–165.

Bakar, O. (2008). The Spiritual and Ethical Foundation of Science and Technology in Islamic Civilisation. *IAIS Journal of Civilisation Studies*, 1(1), 87–112.

Barazangi, N. H. (2008–2009). The Absence of Muslim Women in Shaping Islamic Thought: Foundations of Muslims' Peaceful and Just Co-Existence. *Journal of Law and Religion*, 24(2), 403–432.

Bashkuwal, I. (2008). *Kitab al-Sila fi Ta'rikh A'immat al-Andalus* [Continuation of a Scholarly History of al-Andalus], Vol. 2. Cairo: n.p.

Bataineh, O., Qablan, A., Belbase, S., Takriti, R., & Tairab, H. (2022). Gender Disparity in Science, Technology, Engineering, and Mathematics (STEM) Programs at Jordanian Universities. *Sustainability*, 14(14069), 1–20. https://doi.org/10.3390/su142114069.

Berkey, J. (1992). *The Transmission of Knowledge in Medieval Cairo*. Princeton, N.J.: Princeton University Press.

Bisati, A. A. (2016). Position and Role of Women during the Time of Khulafa'u-Ar-Rashidun. *Insight Islamicus*, 16, 25–42.

Borgerson, K. (2021). Wallada and Hafsa: Gender and Mobility through Medieval Andalusian Poetry. *UCLA Journal of Religion*, 5, 78–89.

Bowman, M. J. & Anderson, C. A. (1980). The Participation of Women in Education in the Third World. *Comparative Education Review*, 24(2), S13–S32.

Brentjes, S., Edis, T., Richter-Bernburg, L. (2016). *1001 Distortions: How (Not) to Narrate History of Science, Medicine, and Technology in Non-western Cultures*. Berlin: Ergon-Verlag GmbH.

Bsoul, L. A. (2018). *Medieval Islamic World: An Intellectual History of Science and Politics*. New York: Peter Lang.

Carullah, M. (2001). *Hatun* [A Woman]. Ankara: Kitabiyat.

Charrad, M. M. (2011). Gender in the Middle East: Islam, State, Agency. *Annual Review of Sociology*, 37, 417–437. www.jstor.org/stable/41288615.

Cherif, F. M. (2010). Culture, Rights, and Norms: Women's Rights Reform in Muslim Countries. *The Journal of Politics*, 72(4), 1144–1160.

Cook, A. (1997). Ladies in the Scientific Revolution. *Notes and Records of the Royal Society of London*, 51(1), 1–12.

Cornell, V. J. (2007). *Voices of Islam*. Westport, CT: Praeger.

Dajani, R., Tabbaa, Z., Al-Rawashdeh, A., Gretzel, U., Bowser, G. (2021). Peer Mentoring Women in STEM: An Explanatory Case Study on Reflections from a Program in Jordan. *Mentoring & Tutoring: Partnership in Learning*, 29(3), 284–304. https://doi.org/10.1080/13611267.2021.1927429.

De Vasconcellos, J. F., Abedalthagafi, M., Calo, S., et al. (2022). Editorial: Women in Science: Genetics. *Frontiers in Genetics*, 13, 1–3. https://doi.org/10.3389/fgene.2022.1038317.

Dodge, B. (1970). *The Fihrist of al-Nadim: A Tenth Century Survey of Muslim Culture*, Vol. 2. New York: Columbia University Press.

Duran, T. (1990). *Deeds of Trust of the Sultans Womenfolk*. Turkey: Tarihi Araştırmalar ve Dokümantasyon Merkezleri Kurma ve Geliştirme Vakfı.

Esposito, J. L. (1975). Women's Rights in Islam. *Islamic Studies*, 14(2), 99–114.

Fish, M. S. (2002). Islam and Authoritarianism. *World Politics*, 55(1), 4–37.

Gaida, M. (2016). Muslim Women and Science: The Search for the 'Missing' Actors. *Early Modern Women: An Interdisciplinary Journal*, 11(1), 197–206.

Gelbart, N. R. (2016). Adjusting the Lens: Locating Early Modern Women of Science. *Early Modern Women: An Interdisciplinary Journal*, 11(1), 116–127.

Gelişli, Y. (2004). Education of Women from the Ottoman Empire to Modern Turkey. *SEER: Journal for Labour and Social Affairs in Eastern Europe*, 7(4), 121–135.

Gorini, R. (2003). Al-Haytham the Man of Experience. First Steps in the Science of Vision. *Journal of the International Society for History of Islamic Medicine*, 2(4), 53–55.

Green, M. H. (2003). History of Science. In Joseph, S., ed., *Encyclopedia of Women and Islamic Cultures*, Vol. 1. Leiden: E. J. Brill, 358–361.

Green, M. H. (2008a). *Making Women's Medicine Masculine: The Rise of Male Authority in Pre-Modern Gynaecology*. Oxford: Oxford University Press.

Green, M. H. (2008b). Conversing with the Minority: Relations among Christian, Jewish, and Muslim Women in the High Middle Ages. *Journal of Medieval History*, 34(2), 105–118.

Günther, S. (2020). *Knowledge and Education in Classical Islam: Religious Learning between Continuity and Change*. Leiden: Brill.

Hambly, G. (1999). *Women in the Medieval Islamic World*. New York: St. Martin's Press.

Hanemann, U. (2015). *Learning Families: Intergenerational Approaches to Literacy Teaching and Learning*. Germany: UNESCO Institute for Lifelong Learning.

Haredy, M. (2020). Women Scholars of *Ḥadīth*: A Case Study of the Eighth/Fourteenth-Century *Muʿjam al-Shaykha Maryam*. In Günther, S., ed.,

Knowledge and Education in Classical Islam: Religious Learning between Continuity and Change, Vol. 2. Leiden: Brill, 908–940.

Hassan, F. (2000). Islamic Women in Science. *Science*, 290 (5489), 55–56.

Hershman, T., Holland, A., & Bell, J. (2021). *On This Day She: Putting Women Back into History, One Day at a Time.* London: Metro.

Hogendijk, J. P. & Sabra, A. I., eds. (2003). *The Enterprise of Science in Islam: New Perspectives.* England: The MIT Press.

Huff, T. (2003). *The Rise of Early Modern Science: Islam, China, and the West*, 2nd ed. Cambridge: Cambridge University Press.

Human Rights Watch. (2018). *Shall I Feed My Daughter, or Educate Her? Barriers to Girls' Education in Pakistan.* New York: Human Rights Watch.

Ibn Sa'd, M. (1957). *Al-Tabaqat al-Kubra.* Beirut: Dar Beirut l-il Tiba'a w-al Nashr.

Issa, A. (1928). *Histoire des Bimaristans a l'Epoque Islamique.* Le Caire: Imprimerie Paul Barbey.

Jagot, S. (2023). Mariam al-Ijli al-Asturlabi (c. Tenth Century CE): An Extract from Fihrist al-Nadim (Index) (c. 998 CE). In Lawrence-Mackey, F., Wills, H., Harrison, S., Jones, E. L., Martin, R., eds., *Women in the History of Science: A Sourcebook.* London: UCL Press, 61–65.

Kahhala, U. R. (1959). *A'lam al-Nisa.* Damascus: Al-Hashimi Press.

Kamali, M. H. (2002). *Freedom, Equality and Justice in Islam.* Malaysia: Ilmiah.

Khalidi, T. (1973). Islamic Biographical Dictionaries: A Preliminary Assessment. *The Muslim World*, 63(1), 53–65.

Khalifa,H. (1941). *Kashf al-Zunun 'an 'Asami al-Kutub wa al-Funun* [The Removal of Doubt from the Names of Books and the Arts]. Istanbul: al-Ma'aref.

Khan, S. A. (2007). *Unveiling the Ideal: A New Look at Early Muslim Women.* Kuala Lumpur: Sisters in Islam.

Keddie, N. R. (2007). *Women in the Middle East: Past and Present.* Princeton, NJ: Princeton University Press.

Keddie, N. R. & Baron, B. (1991). *Women in Middle Eastern History: Shifting Boundaries in Sex and Gender.* New Haven, CT: Yale University Press.

Keddie, N. R. (1990). The Past and Present of Women in the Muslim World. *Journal of World History*, 1(1), 77–108.

Kılıç, A. (2015). *Anadolu Selçuklu ve Osmanlı Şefkat Abideleri: Şifahaneler* [The Şifahanes of Philanthropic Monuments of the Seljuk and Ottoman Eras]. Istanbul: Bilnet Matbaacılık ve Ambalaj A.Ş.

Korkmaz, A. (2021). 'Sabuncuoğlu Şerafeddin Kimdir?' [Who Is Sabuncuoğlu Şerafeddin?], *Sanat Tarihi Platformu*, www.sanattarihiplatformu.com/sabun cuoglu-serafeddin-kimdir392.html#.

Kudsieh, S. (2003). Andalusian Literature: 9th to 15th Century. In Joseph, S., ed., *Encyclopedia of Women and Islamic Cultures*, Vol. 1. Leiden: E. J. Brill, 10–15.

Lehrer, E. L. (1999). Religion as a determinant of educational attainment: An economic perspective. *Social Science Research* 28(4), 358–379.

Lindberg, D. C. (1967). Alhazen's Theory of Vision and Its Reception in the West. *Isis*, 58(3), 321–341.

Majid, A. (1998). The Politics of Feminism in Islam. *Signs: Journal of Women in Culture and Society*, 23(2), 321–389.

Majid, Z. A. (2001). *Lam'ul Isharat Fi Ṭabaqah al-Nisa' al-Faqihat* [The Luminous Signs of the Rank of Women Jurists]. Cairo: Women and Cultural Studies.

Mcclendon, D., Hackett, C., Potančoková, M., Stonawski, M., Skirbekk, V. (2018). Women's Education in the Muslim World. *Population and Development Review*, 44(2), 311–342.

McIntire, S. (2009). *Speeches in World History*. New York: Facts on File Inc.

McKinnon, C. (1982). Feminism, Marxism, Method, and the State: An Agenda for Theory. *Signs*, 7, 515–544.

Merchant, C. (1980). *The Death of Nature: Women, Ecology and the Scientific Revolution*. San Francisco, CA: Harper.

Ministry of Education Malaysia, Educational Planning and Research Division. (2018). *Quick Facts 2018: Malaysia Educational Statistics*. Putrajayam Malaysia: Ministry of Education Malaysia.

Mohammadi, N. & Hazeri, A. M. (2020). Two Different Narratives of Hijab in Iran: Burqa and Niqab. *Sexuality & Culture*, 25, 680–699. https://doi.org/10.1007/s12119-020-09789-3.

Nadwi, M. A. (2013). *Al-Muḥaddithat: The Women Scholars in Islam*. Oxford: Interface.

Naguib, R. (ed.). (2024). *Women's Empowerment and Public Policy in the Arab Gulf States: Exploring Challenges and Opportunities*. Singapore: Springer.

Naguib, R. & Aref, A. (2024). Empowering Women through Public Sector Employment in Qatar: Challenges and Opportunities. In Naguib, R., ed., *Women's Empowerment and Public Policy in the Arab Gulf States: Exploring Challenges and Opportunities*. Singapore: Springer.

Ofek, H. (2011). Why the Arab World Turned Away from Science. *The New Atlantis*, 3. www.thenewatlantis.com/publications/why-the-arabic-world-turned-away-from-science.

Pormann, P. (2009). Female Patients and Practitioners in Medieval Islam. *The Lancet*, 373, 1598–1599.

Pormann, P. E. & Savage-Smith, E. (2007). *Medieval Islamic Medicine*. Washington, D.C.: Georgetown University Press.

Rahman, F. Z. (2012). Gender Equality in Muslim-Majority States and Shari'a Family Law: Is There a Link. *Australian Journal of Political Science*, 47(3), 347–362.

Rizzo, H., Abdel-Latif, A. -H., & Meyer, K. (2007). The Relationship between Gender Equality and Democracy: A Comparison of Arab Versus Non-Arab Muslim Societies. *Sociology*, 41(6), 1151–1170. www.jstor.org/stable/42858291.

Roded, R. (2003). Islamic Biographical Dictionaries: 9th to 10th Centuries. In Joseph, S., ed., *Encyclopedia of Women and Islamic Cultures*, Vol. 1. Leiden: E. J. Brill, 29–31.

Roded, R. (1994). *Women in Islamic Biographical Collections: From Ibn Sa'd to Who's Who*. The United States of America: Lynne Rienner.

Rossiter, M. W. (1974). Women Scientists in America before 1920. *American Scientist*, 62(3), 312–323.

Saliba, G. (2007). *Islamic Science and the Making of the European Renaissance*. Cambridge, MA: The MIT Press.

Sari, N. (2009). Women Dealing with Health during the Ottoman Reign. *Muslim Heritage*, https://muslimheritage.com/women-dealing-with-health-during-the-ottoman-reign.

Sarı, N. (2021). Osmanlı Tıp Tarihi Araştırmalarında Sorunlar. In Bilgin, A. & Aydın, B., eds., *Osmanlı Tarihçiliğine Yön Veren Konuşmalar*. Istanbul: Kronik Kitap, 167–224.

Sarı, N. & İzgöer, A. Z. (2021). Osmanlılarda Kadınlara Mahsus Hastane, Klinik, Koğuş ve Doğumhanelerin Gelişimi. In Bozkurt, F. & Çağlar, B., eds., *İmparatorluğun Son Asrında Osmanlılar*. Istanbul: Kronik Kitap, 217–245.

Schmidl, P. G. (2016). Mirror of the Stars: The Astrolabe and What It Tells about Pre-Modern Astronomy in Islamic Societies. In Brentjes, S., Edis, T., & Richter-Bernburg, L., eds., *1001 Distortions: How (Not) to Narrate History of Science, Medicine, and Technology in non-Western Cultures*. Berlin: Ergon-Verlag GmbH, 173–187.

Scott, S. P. (1904). *The History of the Moorish Empire in Europe*, Vol. 3. Philadelphia, PA: J.B. Lippincott.

Seitkasimova, Z. A. (2019). Status of Women in Ancient Greece. *Open Journal for Anthropological Studies*, 3(2), 49–54.

Sharif, R. (1987). Women in Islam. *European Judaism: A Journal for the New Europe*, 21(1), 28–33.

Siddiqi, M. S. (1982). *The Blessed Women of Islam*. Lahore: Kazi.

Snow, C. P. (1961). *The Two Cultures and the Scientific Revolution*. New York: Cambridge University Press.

Sonbol, A. E. (2003). Rise of Islam: 6th to 9th Century. In Joseph, S., ed., *Encyclopedia of Women and Islamic Cultures*, Vol. 1. Leiden: E. J. Brill, 3–9.

Stewart, A. J. & Winter, D. G. (1977). The Nature and Causes of Female Suppress. *Signs*, 2(3), 531–553.

Surty, M. (1996). *Muslim Contribution to the Development of Hospitals*. Birmingham: Quranic Arabic Foundation.

Suzuki, J. (2009). *Mathematics in Historical Context*. Washington, D.C.: The Mathematical Association of America.

Taskiran, T. (1976). *Women in Turkey*. Istanbul: Redhouse Yayinevi.

Tienxhi, J. Y. (2017). The Gender Gap in Malaysian Public Universities: Examining The 'Lost Boys'. *Journal of International and Comparative Education*, 6(1), 3–18.

Tintori, A. (2017). The Most Common Stereotypes about Science and Scientists: What Scholars Know. In Tintori, A. & Palomba, R., eds. *Turn on the Light on Science*. London: Ubiquity Press. https://doi.org/10.5334/bba.b. License: CC-BY 4.0, pp. 1–18.

Ullmann, M. (1978). *Islamic Medicine*. Edinburg: Edinburg University Press.

UNESCO. (2015). *UNESCO Science Report: Towards 2030*. Luxembourg: UNESCO.

UNESCO Office Bangkok and Regional Bureau for Education in Asia and the Pacific. (2015). *Closing the Gender Gap in STEM: Drawing More Girls and Women into Science, Technology, Engineering and Mathematics*. Thailand: UNESCO Bangkok.

Usaybi'a, I. A. (1998). *Essential Sources of Information on the Classes of Physicians*. Beirut: Dar al-Thaqafah.

Vila, A. C. (1995). Sex and Sensibility: Pierre Roussel's Système physique et moral de la femme. *Representations*, *52*, 76–93. https://doi.org/10.2307/2928700.

Villar, P. & Guppy, N. (2015). Gendered Science: Representational Dynamics in British Columbia Science Textbooks over the Last Half Century. *Canadian Journal of Education / Revue canadienne de l'éducation*, 38(3), 1–24.

Waddy, C. (1980). *Women in Muslim History*. Great Britain: Longman.

Whaley, L. (2011). *Women and the Practice of Medical Care in Early Modern Europe, 1400–1800*. Basingstoke: Palgrave Macmillan.

White, J. B. (2003). State Feminism, Modernisation, and the Turkish Republican Woman. *NWSA Journal*, 15(3), 145–159.

WIPO. (2021). *Global Innovation Index 2021: Tracking Innovation through the COVID-19 Crisis*. Geneva: World Intellectual Property Organisation.

Yermolenko, G. (2005). Roxolona: The Greatest Empresse of the East. *The Muslim World*, 95(2), 231–248.

Youssef, N. H. (1976–1977). Education and Female Modernism in the Muslim World. *Journal of International Affairs*, 30(2), 191–209.

Zainuddin, A. A. & Mahdy, Z. A. (2017). The Islamic Perspectives of Gender-Related Issues in the Management of Patients with Disorders of Sex Development. *Archives of Sexual Behavior*, 46(2), 353–360. https://doi.org/10.1007/s10508-016-0754-y.

Cambridge Elements=

Islam and the Sciences

Nidhal Guessoum
American University of Sharjah, United Arab Emirates

Nidhal Guessoum is Professor of Astrophysics at the American University of Sharjah, United Arab Emirates. Besides Astrophysics, he has made notable contributions in Science & Islam/ Religion, education, and the public understanding of science; he has published books on these subjects in several languages, including *The Story of the Universe* (in Arabic, first edition in 1997), *Islam's Quantum Question* (in English in 2010, translated into several languages), and *The Young Muslim's Guide to Modern Science* (in English 2019, translated into several languages), numerous articles (academic and general-public), and vast social-media activity.

Stefano Bigliardi
Al Akhawayn University in Ifrane, Morocco

Stefano Bigliardi is Associate Professor of Philosophy at Al Akhawayn University in Ifrane, Morocco. He trained as a philosopher of science, has a PhD in philosophy from the University of Bologna, and has been serving in different positions at universities in Germany, Sweden, Mexico, and Switzerland. He has published a monograph and a general-public book on Islam and Science as well as dozens of articles (peer-reviewed and popular) on the subject and others. Since 2016, he has taught undergraduate courses on Islam and Science at Al Akhawayn University in Ifrane, Morocco.

About the Series

Elements in Islam and the Sciences is a new platform for the exploration, critical review and concise analysis of Islamic engagements with the sciences: past, present and future. The series will not only assess ideas, arguments and positions; it will also present novel views that push forward the frontiers of the field. These Elements will evince strong philosophical, theological, historical, and social dimensions as they address interactions between Islam and a wide range of scientific subjects.

Cambridge Elements=

Islam and the Sciences

Elements in the Series

Islam and Science: Past, Present, and Future Debates
Nidhal Guessoum and Stefano Bigliardi

Islam's Encounter with Modern Science: A Mismatch Made in Heaven
Taner Edis

Islam and Environmental Ethics
Muhammad Yaseen Gada

Islam, Causality, and Science: Perspectives on Reconciliation of Islamic Tradition and Modern Science
Özgür Koca

Muslim Women in Science, Past and Present
Elmira Akhmetova

A full series listing is available at: www.cambridge.org/EISC

For EU product safety concerns, contact us at Calle de José Abascal, 56–1°,
28003 Madrid, Spain or eugpsr@cambridge.org.

www.ingramcontent.com/pod-product-compliance
Ingram Content Group UK Ltd.
Pitfield, Milton Keynes, MK11 3LW, UK
UKHW020046160325
456256UK00019B/510